Finding PASSION AND PURPOSE
IN FAITH, FAMILY AND VOCATION

LIVING *the*
ABUNDANT
LIFE

ROGER WELDON

TABLE OF CONTENTS

This is the true job in life,
the being used for a purpose
recognized by yourself as a mighty one;
the being a force of nature
instead of a feverish selfish little clod of ailments and
grievances complaining that the world will not devote
itself to making you happy.

I want to be thoroughly used up when I die,
for the harder I work the more I live.
I rejoice in life for its own sake.

Life is no brief candle to me.
It is a sort of splendid torch
which I have a hold of for the moment,
and I want to make it burn as brightly as possible before
handing it on to future generations.

(George Bernard Shaw)

ACKNOWLEDGEMENTS

To those in my immediate family whose contributions have been so instrumental:

Beth – my beautiful wife ~ For allowing me to live without masks (though that is not always a pretty sight), for your unconditional love for our family and your modeling of what loving God, your spouse, your children and your neighbor should look like.

Emily, Raymond, and Ethan – our beautiful gifts from God ~ For the right to be called the most wonderful name I can imagine: "Daddy." There is no greater joy in life than hearing that name directed at me from your lips and feeling the love conveyed by your frequent hugs. I love you all so much and cannot wait to see the amazing things that God is going to do through your life.

Earl Weldon Jr – my Dad ~ It has been 22 years since you left and I so look forward to the day when we will meet again. In so many ways you still influence me today. None are as important as the realization I have gained as I have aged and become a father myself. I now see more clearly how very much you loved me and wanted me to be all that I was designed to be. I have grown to be a man but still swell with pride when I return home, where I am known as your son.

Melba Weldon – my Mother ~ A Mother's influence on a son's life cannot be overstated. I will never recover from all of the times you have said to me, "Roger, I am so proud of you." This statement from you, uttered at times when I did and did not feel worthy, has always reminded me of both who I was and who I should be.

Raymond Fiveash – my boss, my friend, my mentor, my Dad after I had lost my own ~ As a young man I learned to believe in myself because you believed in me. A son of mine bears your name, in part, because I never would have been worthy of being his father but for your influence in my life. I look forward to laughing with you again.

Connie Rayne – my mother-in-law, my friend ~ For your constant encouragement through this project and incredible modeling of what it looks like to be passionately in love with Jesus.

To the many others whose contributions added so much to this book and my life:

Bryan Collier – my Pastor, my friend ~ For your feedback, assistance, time, and affirmation. For believing during the most vulnerable period of the vision God placed on my heart. Most of all for your incredible example of what a Pastor, friend, leader, husband, father, and fully-surrendered Christ follower can and should look like. "You're not sick, you don't have a problem … God wired you that way!" The Kingdom will be much more crowded because of your response to the call.

Chad Barker ~ for that ride back from Birmingham when you affirmed my vision and challenged it at the same time. If the vision bears fruit for the Kingdom, it will be in no small part because you challenged me to do what God was calling me to do.

Louis Holmes ~ "As iron sharpens iron so one man sharpens another" (Prov 27:17). I continue to learn what Christ-centered fatherhood should look like from your example.

To those who reviewed all or portions of the project or have helped form it, in some way, through the years:

Bryan Collier, Louis Holmes, Jennifer Johnson, Connie Rayne, John Perry, Paul Holbrook, Candi Johnson, Ron

Living the Abundant Life

Bouthillette, Guy Richardson, J.T. Washington, Arthur DuCote, John Shackleford.

To The Orchard in Tupelo, Mississippi – Staff, members, and those who call The Orchard their church home. For your fellowship and for allowing me a glimpse of how God surely intended the Body of Christ to function on earth.

To Cher and Bil Holton – for your delightful partnering and assistance in converting this from a "project" into a book. I could not have imagined a better fit for this work or a more professional, enjoyable process. Thank you!

Finally ... but first. Thank you Jesus for bringing people into my life who would constantly redirect me toward You. For letting me see what life is like apart from You and for not rescuing me from the brokenness before I truly learned the emptiness of that separation. For bringing me home and letting me feel the power inherent in being a child of the King. For lighting me on fire and sustaining the burn. For loving me. In giving me more of Yourself, you have given me all that I need. It is enough.

A NOTE TO THE READER

This book is for believers. It is for believers in faith, believers in hope, believers in love. It is for those who believe in today and tomorrow. It is for those who believe in the wonderful promises of Jesus. It is for those who believe in the life Jesus promised. Life – life more abundantly. It is not only written *for* these believers, but *because* too many believers are living in crisis.

We are experiencing a crisis in our lives; a crisis in our country; a crisis in our faith. Our crisis, though, is not one of a foreign invader or an external threat. Rather, our crisis is internal. Our crisis is that we are losing our ability to believe. We have lost contact with our internal compass. We're searching for True North and aren't sure how to get our bearings.

I was on the bridge of a U.S. Navy warship when I first began to understand the nature of our crisis. As a Naval Officer standing constant Bridge watches, navigation was near and dear to me during this period of my life. The perils of the Persian Gulf, with its shallow waters, hazards to navigation, oil wells, and small craft activity, were very real. So I tended to spend a great deal of time at the navigation chart table talking with sailors responsible for assisting the Bridge team with navigation.

Above the chart table was the Global Positioning System (GPS) into which we programmed key points in our journey. For some masochistic reason we also added the coordinates for our homeport of Pearl Harbor, Hawaii. So the tendency on slow watches in the middle of the night was to check the navigation picture and do one additional turn on GPS to see how far from home we were. It was a painful practice – 8,000 miles from home one moment, 8,032 miles a few hours later; 8,015 one day, 8,016 the next. In other words, we were going nowhere fast – in accordance with the plan.

At some point during that journey I reflected on just what the virtually unchanging mileage read-out on GPS meant to me. As a husband and father it meant I had to struggle to keep my spirits up during a difficult period of separation. Day and night I gazed at the pictures of my family. It was their pictures, their letters, their e-mail, the memories, that gave me hope for the future and a reason to keep going. At the same time though, they almost paralyzed me with anguish because I missed my family so terribly.

As a leader I had to look at the mental and physical effects of our environment on those I led. Maintaining performance standards with a crew of young, overworked, and underpaid sailors was never easy. Add to that the fact that they were 8,000 miles from home and would not see their loved ones for six months, and you have quite a dilemma. How can you keep them motivated? How can you get them to practice fire drills enthusiastically, four times in one week, when they were battling homesick feelings, depression, lack of sleep, and 115 degree temperatures? How can you even get them to care?

The real learning experience for me, though, was considering how to keep living, smiling, loving life and looking forward to tomorrow, when tomorrow just represented more of the same.

What I discovered was that when you are 8,000 miles from home, with months left until you return and a high-stress job full of redundancy, you couldn't count on your job to provide you with a reason for living. Conversely, if you tried to go through the motions until you returned home you were going to be disappointed. Life will never be satisfied with the constraints of work, nor will it be duped into waiting for a tomorrow that may never come.

Sadly, I saw so many young sailors come aboard full of life and enthusiasm only to slowly pull away and disengage from life. The long hours, heat, pressure and redundancy took their toll and these young servicemen would literally stop caring. Though they would not verbalize it, their actions and attitudes conveyed their dissatisfaction so clearly. They were four months and 8,000 miles from home, and they just didn't care.

"Lock me up, beat me, whatever, I just want to go home" was their unstated but clearly communicated refrain.

Life throughout America is just like life on that ship in many respects. We kiss our children as we walk out the door, whispering an encouraging word and wishing them a great day. We get in our car, tolerate a short drive to work, and end up in a world that may as well be 8,000 miles from home. We enter a world of monotony where we work hard all day, but are often left feeling that we have been totally unproductive. Confronted with small problems and seemingly urgent issues every day, we do our best to solve those issues that are brought before us. In so doing we attempt to mend organizational fences and put out the proverbial brushfires that wreak so much havoc. We attend meetings, more meetings and more meetings. We tackle the endless stream of paperwork and create more efficient ways of organizing our inbox. Tied to our desk and laptop, we busy ourselves sending e-mail after e-mail and congratulating ourselves for mastering our monotony.

Meanwhile, it has been so long since we gave our all, or wore ourselves out over something meaningful, that we have forgotten how good it feels to be fully engaged with life. Instead we defend the status quo and our contribution to it. At some point we must realize that the mooring lines have been cast off and land is nowhere in sight. We are "8,000 miles" from home and going in the wrong direction. The course we plotted was planned in good faith, but we can no longer deny the sneaking suspicion that we have missed our port of call and often drift aimlessly in the changing currents of life.

We are pleased with our title and opportunities for promotion, but deep down inside we wonder what is missing. Or maybe we are *not* satisfied with our career progress but seem unaffected by the feeling that it does not seem to matter as much as it did before. We mastered the art of being comfortably dissatisfied. Either way we know that we don't feel complete. Our titles, promotions and even the money have lost their charm. Unfortunately we have been traveling in one direction for so long that we don't even know how to reverse course. And we surely don't know what we would do once we turned the "vessel" in the right direction – whatever that direction might be.

Meanwhile, something within us stirs as we sit through sermons and hear of the wonderful promises of our Lord. Joy, fulfillment, life everlasting, life more abundant – all of the things we are searching for. We participate in the worship services because they lift our spirits and give us hope. Though we grow in our faith walk, we also grow more keenly aware of our lack of satisfaction with our Monday through Friday, 9-to-5 existence. The two just don't fit together and while one helps provide meaning, most of our time is spent at the other.

Consider for a moment the words to the Steven Curtis Chapman song *The Change*. "What about the change? What about the difference? What about the grace? What about forgiveness? What about a life that's showing I'm undergoing the change."

What has changed?
I know you are forgiven.
I know you are saved.
I know you are loved.
But what has really changed?

What can you point to and say, "Here is God in me? Here is an unmistakable sign of His hand in my life?" Show me an area of your life where you are bulletproof; where you walk without fear; where you trample over critics and those who try to get you off your path – the destination God placed before you.

Tell me of that path. Tell me of that certainty. Tell me of the confidence that comes from knowing that you walk with God and that you know Him. Tell me of the confidence and pleasure it gives you to say you are doing exactly what God put you on the face of the earth to do.

Living the Abundant Life

Let me see the passion in your eyes as you explain that life is more than just walking around and sucking up other people's air. Show me that it is a gift allocated to you and that you have specific things to accomplish, things designed by God Himself, while you are here on earth.

Watch me marvel at your confidence when your activities today, not in a distant and murky tomorrow, relate directly to the reason God put you here.

See my eyes light up as I recognize the hand of God on your life. Can I see the sign of someone marked by a relationship and a calling from the Creator of the Universe? Do I see someone with the accoutrements of religion, or do I see a person consumed by the fire that God put within his or her heart? Am I standing before a person who has a clear understanding of what the Creator wants to do with that fire? Someone like John the Baptist perhaps, or Joshua, or Moses, who was "arrested at the sign of a bush, burning yet not burned up – as if God were telling him from the very beginning that his call would set his life on fire, but the fire would not consume him." [1]

What is it that so consumes you? What is your burning bush? What is it that, when you are doing it, makes you think the world is unfolding just as it should? What is it that makes you think that if you do nothing else but this, God will be satisfied with your life?

What is it that makes you say, "What I do is me. For this I came?"[2] What could you do that would make you say that? What is it that could make you claim that doing it represents your essence, and that the activity, service, or function is the reason you were born?

If today were your last day on earth what would you point to as a sign of a life well lived? If God were to ask what you did with what He gave you, what your contribution to the Kingdom was, how would you answer?

In John 10:10, Jesus said "I have come that they may have life, and that they may have it more abundantly." You live, you breathe. But do you live an abundant life? Is your cup so full that it overflows? Do you live an abundant life – by His standards? Does your laugh get stronger and more frequent with age? Does the twinkle in your eyes grow brighter, your sense of humor improve? Do you have the joy that He spoke of?

Can you say without a doubt that you know why you are here?

"What I do is me. For this I came."

Can you make that statement your own?

If there is doubt, if there is uncertainty, if you have not found the *this* in "For this I came," then welcome to the club. You are in good company because most of those who are alive today are members. Most people have not figured out what the *this* is!

Now, let's take a trip together. The purpose of the journey is to leave the club and find the *this* in "For this I came." When we really get serious about living the abundant life that Jesus promised we might have, we have to determine why He put us here to begin with. That starts with understanding that we are not a cosmic accident. We are not simply the product of reproductive forces. Each of us is a part of a game plan that God is executing on the face of the earth. We have the opportunity to get off the bench and score a few points for a Coach whose favor knows no bounds and whose encouragement is worthy of our life.

Take abundant living seriously and you will find fruitfulness of a magnitude never before imagined. When you come to understand that you are a major player in God's grand scheme, you will no longer be satisfied with not knowing or doing your part. No longer satisfied with getting by. No longer satisfied with the status quo.

You also may not be so disturbed by the things that now disturb you so much. The small become miniscule and the irritants are suddenly not worthy of conversation. The unimportant fades to the background as your purpose for being transforms your life into something so powerful that you cannot imagine how you lived before.

Come with me on that journey. I have been there and I am still traveling that path each day. I am overwhelmed by the feelings that come from my ability to say that I am doing exactly what God put me on the face of the earth to do. Today, tomorrow, forever!

 And my life is dedicated to helping you say the same thing.
For this I came.

INTRODUCTION

I started developing this material because of my passion for the topic of leadership. Time and time again I have seen that it is leadership that makes the difference. Whether an organization suffers or succeeds – corporate, sports, non-profit, church, or even a family – it is probably attributable to the leader and his or her influence.

I have had a passion for leadership since my early days in the U.S. Navy. It was so easy to see those who had "it" and those who did not – those who realized that it was people who made the process work – whatever that process might be. Those were the people we all wanted to serve with and under – we were willing to pay the price for that type of leader.

Years later as I continued to explore the subject I realized that we are not really looking for great leaders after all. Granted, we like being led and we love being led well. Having a healthy respect or admiration for the one we work for can add significantly to the quality of our life. But believing in a great boss or organization is not nearly as important as maintaining the ability to believe in something.

It is easy to point to the organizations that have crumbled and say that their demise underwrites our lack of belief. Priests are being accused and convicted of unutterable acts; major companies are inflating earnings and hiding the truth. The cost is not solely in dollars and cents, it is in the lost retirement funds and reduced quality of life of the very people who worked hard to make the company a success. Corporate CEO's, top government officials, and lobbyists create new languages of denial and deceit in our country, while unscrupulous leaders in other countries export terrorism. Every few years millionaire athletes talk about going on strike while minimum wage workers pay $50 per month cable bills to watch them play a game. Each side of the congressional fence points to the other as the reason more progress is not being made. Clearly all is not well!

These difficulties though are not the reason for our crisis of belief. They are the symptoms. Our crisis of belief exists because we as individuals are often unclear about who we are, where we are going, or why we are here to begin with. Amidst the frantic pace of our lives, we pause to wonder if this is really all that life is about. We ask ourselves what difference we are making. We need to believe our life has some significance – that our life matters. Too often, however, we stop believing that we have a significant role in the world and in the lives of others. The affirmation that our life is a splendid torch burning brightly for all to see and for the glory of God often seems to be in short supply. Without this affirmation we lose sight of the fact that we were put here to impact the world and the Kingdom of God in extraordinary ways. We stop believing.

So if Jesus came so that we would have life, abundant life, then our lives and our contributions are far from being as they were intended to be. Let me share some insights I learned from a few of my previous work experiences that might illustrate these points more clearly.

WORKING IN A PAWNSHOP

When I was 16 years old I was fortunate enough to work in an incredibly interesting business with an amazing man. Raymond Fiveash was a pawnbroker and had spent 40 years in the pawnshop business. During that time he learned a little about virtually everything. He knew about guns, jewelry, musical instruments and electronics. He was an expert in a wide variety of topics. More importantly, he was an expert in human beings and taught me more about people than anyone I have ever known.

I became a good "people watcher." If someone pawned a gold ring, I would watch them, listen to them, hear what they said and did not say. When someone brought in a gun, I watched them. I asked them questions. Did they know enough about it to prove they owned it?

The subtle things people said and did were often clear windows into their life. I witnessed the elation over a newfound job and the pride of a pawn ticket redeemed. I saw the despair in someone's eyes who walks through the door after his job has been eliminated, but whose children still need to eat. I've observed hands weighed down with merchandise as a customer backs through the door and desperately looks for an empathetic reception that will indicate that all hope is not lost.

Amidst the coming and going, merchandise being brought in, picked up, or simply left behind, there was the constant rub that "this just isn't the way it was supposed to turn out." The wedding ring comes off the finger so a family can eat next week. The couple shake their heads in amazement and despair wondering: "How did we get to this point?" Etched on their faces is the look that says: "Tomorrow holds no promises – no hope – that will improve upon today."

SERVING ON A NAVY WARSHIP

A community of sailors on one of the Navy's newest warships represents a true cross section of society. I observed young men from all walks of life come aboard the ship. They seemed full of life and in earnest anticipation for what the future would hold.

A 19-year-old raised his right hand and solemnly swore to "support and defend the Constitution of the United States against all enemies, foreign and domestic ..." just two months after his high school graduation. Full of dreams of adventure and pride in what he will do for his country, he embarked upon his military journey.

Two years later, his journey takes him to the first downtown district off a Navy pier that sells cold beer. His dreams and pride have been replaced by coldness and bitterness. Although his commitment to his country makes him a hero, something inside him has died. His dreams have been replaced by silent despair. He covers it well but there is a deep disappointment that comes from dreams that failed to materialize the way he imagined they would. The glamour and adventure of overseas ports faded against a backdrop of rust removal, late night watches, monotony, and seasoned veterans who scoffed at his dreams. "That's not the way it is in the real world" he was told.

It wasn't long before he believed them. "No more foolish dreams," he told himself, "no more irrational hopes." He ends up just getting by, day by day, pretending that everything is okay. All the while he senses that something is just not right. He embodies a description from John Eldredge's book, *The Journey of Desire*:

> *Everyone else seems to be getting on with things. What's wrong with me? We feel guilty about our chronic disappointment. Why can't I just learn to be happier in my job, in my marriage, in my church, in my group of friends? You see, even while we are doing other things, "getting on with life," we still have an eye out for the life we secretly want.* [1]

So he keeps following the lead of others who are getting on with life. He listens to their wise counsel to reach for something more moderate than the stars. Pretty soon he doesn't have to contend with those dreams at all. They no longer haunt him because he has simply stopped dreaming. He settles into a "getting by" existence and revels in the comfort of mediocrity.

But during those midnight watches, when he spends hours looking upon the sea, he is tortured by the majestic serenity of the moonlit sea before him and the stark contrast between that scene and his life. He reflects on his life and is saddened by his thoughts. He is worldly, he is tough, he is getting along just fine, but he knows that where he is was not where he planned to be.

His was to be a significant role, even a hero's part, but now he just gets by – he survives. He can hide it from others but cannot lie to himself. Inside he knows this is not how it was all supposed to turn out and he is desperate to find the way to somewhere, anywhere, other than where he is. But he has no

Living the Abundant Life

idea where to start, so he just continues to go through the motions and slips further with each passing day from where he needs to be.

WORKING IN A MENTAL HOSPITAL

They came, day and night, and in different stages of required intervention. Some had to be watched and managed very carefully to ensure their safety. Others came confused and scared. Still others came broken, defeated, battered by the gusts of adversity and turbulent seas of life. They couldn't take any more so they retreated to a safe inner harbor to dock their souls.

As days went by they would adjust to the society within the hospital, and it was my job to talk with them, take vitals, and "chart" our discussions. Again and again I was struck by the fact that these were not crazed lunatics, but good people who were simply down and out and desperately in need of help. The events that triggered their breaking point usually did not appear to be dramatic or life changing from an outsider's perspective. The cause of their retreat could have been an argument; it could have been precipitated by something they saw or heard; it could have been something they were thinking. Something about these things sent them "over the edge" and caused them to end up in the hospital. To most people, these events might not have even caused a bad day. But to these people the events they experienced were literally life-altering.

Why would they have been dismantled by seemingly ordinary events when others might not be? Some would argue that the cause would be physiological; others would say psychological; still others would believe brain chemistry or a break down caused their hospitalization. The answers are beyond my explanations.

But this I know: Some triggering event was the final straw that broke the camel's back as the saying goes. When these people entered the hospital the common mood was not rage, or blistering anger, it was a sense of helplessness, of defeat, of despair so deep that it created an emotional vacuum in their life.

Each day they sat there in front of me, slumped over. The life had literally been sucked out of them. Their hollow eyes, lacking even a glimmer of hope, were devoid of all light. Their demeanors posed their questions louder and with more clarity than mere words could articulate: "How did I get here? How did it come to this? How can there be a tomorrow? Where am I? Who am I?"

WORKING IN A BANK

The irony was incredible. I worked at a branch bank in a very affluent area in Southwest Florida. Next to the bank was a retirement community that housed many "snowbirds" – Northerners who had purchased a Florida home and spent their winters there. These good people generally lived a life of relative affluence after spending their working years building a nest egg for a golden, active retirement period. While I enjoyed meeting so many good-hearted, good-natured people from that retirement community, there was another impression that was more telling.

The number of people in that community who lived bitter, angry lives still haunts me. So many were shrouded with negativity and cynicism, and poisoned others with their destructive emotions. Although they were financially set, they seemed to have everything except happiness and peace.

These people spent their entire lives believing in a false premise: "If we can just make it to Florida with a nice nest egg in the bank, we will be okay, and we can really enjoy life." The problem was, many times the "we" was not a "we" anymore. Sometimes a spouse grew tired of the journey and checked out of the marriage before the golden years arrived, not content to wait for the good life any longer. Other times, tragically, a spouse died and left the architect of the grand retirement scheme with no one to enjoy it with and no sense of purpose in life. Frequently, these people focused their last 20-25 working years on their comfortable retirement only to get there and ask, "Is this it?" They were angry at life for not providing the contentment they so longed for. Life, meanwhile, kept asking the question "Why did you wait? I was there all along and you ignored me."

Do you know people like that? Does any of this sound familiar? Many of these people had material and financial wealth but they also had horrible emptiness inside of them. They were hollow inside and you could see and sense it from the moment you met them.

They, too, asked the questions: "Is this it? Is this the way it was supposed to be? Is this all that I was supposed to do with my life?"

ATTENDING CHURCH

For almost two decades his leadership had been *the* leadership at the church. In fact, it was his leadership that started the church, burned the first mortgage, and escorted the congregation through those significant milestones in the life of a young church which grew to a membership of 1200.

Unfortunately, at some point the vision for the church became his vision, not God's. Associate Pastors began to come and go, most with good promise coming in, all escorted out by the hosts of negativity and animosity. He surrounded himself with people who adored him and refused to give audience to anyone who opposed his vision for the future. As that vision lost its clarity and the absence of God's presence became obvious, more people left the church. Both the old and the young, the past as well as the future, were being sacrificed.

Finally he retires, leaving the membership divided, depleted and stagnant. But the story does not end there. Unable to let go of the drugs of adoration and acclaim, he undermines his successor at every turn. He anticipates the phone call asking him to ride in on his white horse and save the church from those he deems unworthy to continue his unproductive, atrophied, and self-centered legacy.

The call does not come, of course, but confrontation does. His subterfuge is exposed and he is forcefully ejected from any association with his old congregation. He had turned a life in service to God into a self-serving ministry.

Can you imagine him asking of the church, himself, or even God: "What went wrong? How could it end like this? Is this all there is to it? How did I get here?"

THE RECURRING QUESTIONS

These examples highlight the questions people sometimes ask when tragedy strikes or life fails to unfold as it should. The reality is that we all face a similar series of questions as we go through life.

Quietly, to ourselves and perhaps to a few trusted friends, we wonder ...

> *Is this all there is to my journey?*
> *Is this all I was put here to do?*
> *Will I live the rest of my life just like this?*
> *Will I make a difference?*
> *Do I matter?*

At the heart of such wondering is another question: Who am I and why am I here? We typically start hearing *the question* late in our teens or early twenties. During these formative years we are filled with idealism and truly think we can change the world.

Then something happens. We start a family. We go to work. We settle down. Our idealism either gets crushed out of us by nay-sayers or pushed out of us because of our busyness. We don't have time to change the world because there are organizations to run or diapers to change or mortgages to pay.

So we settle into a routine that we could justify as reasonable, rational, and unselfish. We stop thinking only of ourselves and turn our focus to others. We grow up and learn to put responsibilities like the mortgage, work, family, health, and education before our dream. We justify it on the altar of self-sacrifice and claim that we are doing it for our family. Not only do we forget *about* our dreams – we forget *how* to dream.

Consequently we dismiss our dream and forget we were made for a world changing purpose. Our own very special purpose gets lost in the shuffle, lost in the confusion, lost in the troubles and cares of this world, lost in the noise ... just lost.

Still, this special stirring will not leave us alone, despite our attempts to deny its presence. We put on our mask and paste on our smile and go through our routines. With great effort we can almost get the questions to stop. We try to drown out the noise by keeping ourselves distracted. We can almost pass our routine off for the real thing. Almost. But not quite.

But joy eludes us. Purpose evades our grasp. Significance hides around corners just outside of sight. The true peace that we seek, "the peace of God, which surpasses all understanding" (Phil 4:6-7), cannot be found. And we will continue to live without these things until we answer the following question: Who am I?

Am I the same person at home as I am at work? The same at church as I am at home and work? If I'm not, have I answered the question?

Who am I?

What is the source of my satisfaction? Whose approval do I need to feel like I have accomplished something? What needs are fulfilled by my striving to please someone the way I do? What needs are fulfilled if I conform or rebel?

Who am I?

Is there a God who loves me? Can He really love me after all I have done? Can I grasp that He loves me and that I will be with Him forever? What does He want from me? He says I am His workmanship, His fellow worker who has been given unique gifts and talents. What am I supposed to do with these gifts? Do I even believe I have sufficient talents? Do I believe I have been uniquely gifted?

Who am I?

The world sings these inquiries like a refrain.

Who am I?
We change our hair, our eye color, our body weight and
shape.
Who am I?
We change our job, our church, our spouse,
our car, our home.
Who am I?
We change our mind, our priorities, our broker.
Who am I?
We build our nest egg, our empire, our reputation. We
become ill-adjusted robots, of sorts, moving here and
there but going nowhere.
Who am I?
Do I do anything more than create a disturbance in
the earth's electromagnetic field by my activity?

Who is the person who sits back in that easy chair,
thumbing through the channels, talking about dinner,
talking about the weekend, talking about nothing? Who is
this person, who in all of his earnestness and sincerity
finds himself –

Wondering,
   Waiting,
      Hoping,
         Praying,
Wasting away,
   Asking please,
      Please,
         Don't,
            Let THIS be it!
Who Am I?

If you have felt that call, that inner stirring to find out who
you really are, this book is for you. If you have found yourself
adrift with thoughts that your life is a narrative without a plot,
this book is for you. In essence, this book is about your calling,
your destiny, your fate.

All of us enter the world called. We are created in the image of God as His most cherished of creations. He calls us by name as an intimate Father to His children.

All of us enter the world with purpose. We are assured that our lives have purpose and that we are created by God to do magnificent work – Kingdom work – while here on earth.

The calling, the purpose, the passion that underlies a life lived in such a manner. These are the certainties of the life we are promised by God. But so often these things are viewed as intangibles, things that cannot be touched and seen, things that may not be relevant in the real world.

This book is written to help make these things relevant. True life, abundant life, is not a life wrapped up in the realities of the world as presented by the world. Abundant life is dominated by an overriding sense of connection with God who created the world and all things in it to act in accordance with His designs. It is only when we find those designs for our life that we will truly be home, truly live abundantly.

This book is written to help you live the abundant life – to help you find out why you are here. It is my sincere hope that by the time you flip to the last page, you will be able to exclaim with confidence and joy:

"THIS IS WHAT I MUST DO. THIS IS WHO I AM. FOR THIS I CAME!"

PERSONAL REFLECTIONS

Write a brief answer to the following questions:

Is the life you are living the life you dreamed about? Why or why not? Explain.

Do you ever wonder, "Is this it? Is this all there is to life?"

Have you ever asked yourself, "Who am I?" Write your own description of who you think you are. You can record your thoughts in narrative form, or simply jot down ideas as they come.

1

How Did This Happen?

Our wanderings and wonderings lead to questions intertwined one with another. "Who am I" is tossed out, though with less frequency than the safer questions: "What is it that I'm supposed to do with my life? Am I in the wrong field of work? Is this really what I'm going to be doing forever? Can I take another week of this? Can I take another week with him or her?" Though different in text and context, these questions emanate from the same place deep within each of us. John Eldredge asks similar questions in his book *The Journey of Desire*:

> *How about your work, your place in the world? Do you go to bed each night with a deep sense of having made a lasting contribution? Do you enjoy ongoing recognition for your unique successes? Are you working in a field that fits you? Are you working at all? What if I told you that this is how it will always be, that this life as you now experience it will go on forever just as it is, without improvement of any kind? Your health will stay as it is. Your finances will remain as they are, your relationships, your work, all of it. It is hell.*
>
> *By the grace of God, we cannot quite pull it off. In the quiet moments of the day we sense a nagging within, a discontent, a hunger for something else. But*

*because we have not solved the riddle of our existence,
we assume that something is wrong – not with life, but
with us.*[1]

The questions we are asking do not deal with whether
there is emptiness within us – there is. The questions are:
Where does it come from? How did it get there? How do the
dreams of our youth – such a big part of our young life –
completely fade from our thoughts and decision-making
process? How do we just stop dreaming altogether? How is it
that we find ourselves living a life that is not reflective of the
abundant life that Jesus said He came to provide? How did
this happen?

Our emptiness may be the result of distance from God and
our innate need to live in relationship with Him. We will never
be whole apart from that relationship. For those who bear the
title "Christian" but still feel incomplete, the emptiness may
be the result of knowing Him but not living the life He
prescribed when He said: "I have come that they may have
life, and that they may have it more abundantly" (Jn 10:10).
What is it that keeps us from living in such a manner?

I propose to you that there are six factors which divert us
from living the abundant life. These factors make us forget our
dreams, our uniqueness in this world, and our purpose.
Though these six are not intended to be exhaustive, I see them
at play so frequently that they must be mentioned. They
represent everything from the intentional undermining of you
and your dreams to the subtle yet unintentional means by
which the world, even people you love, will take the wind out
of your sails.

The factors that keep us from living a victorious, joy-filled,
abundant life are ambient noise, lack of modeling, fear of
rejection, fear in general, exhaustion, and settling. Let us delve
into each and consider their impact on our life, our dreams,
and our journey toward abundance.

Living the Abundant Life

AMBIENT NOISE

The face of Anti-Submarine Warfare has changed dramatically over the years. We are all accustomed to seeing a sonar operator sitting on a ship or submarine listening intently for any sounds in the ocean that might indicate a foreign submarine in the area. For example, the sonar operator in *The Hunt for Red October* engrosses us as he uses his keen auditory senses to identify the Soviet submarine.

In reality, much of Anti-Submarine Warfare these days is done without the use of headphones or humans listening to anything. Instead, sonar domes and towed arrays are used to listen to all of the frequencies in the water. These frequencies are transferred to a bar graph of sorts that is displayed visually on a panel in front of the sonar operator. The operator must look at the frequencies, displayed as lines on the graph, and determine which frequencies are valid and which are not. Operators must distinguish which frequencies represent the ambient noise of the sea – sea life, friendly vessels, cooks preparing food in the galley – from those frequencies that identify a hostile submarine or torpedo doors opening.

The secret lies in the ability to differentiate the noise that represents a threat from all of the other noise. In the Navy we used what we called the "Big Ocean theory," which suggested that in all likelihood you will not run into another ship at sea because there's just a whole lot of sea out there. The same applies to ambient noise when looking for submarines. There is so much noise in the ocean, so much that is causing frequencies to be generated and propagated through the water, that it is incredibly difficult to detect one critical frequency line if it is really there.

You get so used to all of the irrelevant noise that you might not believe something is there when it really is. You may not believe your eyes when you see a line that indicates a real threat because you are so accustomed to seeing only ambient noise which means nothing and requires no action.

The seductive power of "ambient noise" in our life is incredibly strong and can wreak havoc on our dreams. At some point most of us had a dream, a focus, an ideal life we were striving for. This dream represented the "frequency line" we were looking for. For a time our "internal sonar" sets were probably tuned to that frequency with precision. There was so much going on in our world yet we were focused on that one thing because it was what commanded our attention and our commitment.

Then something happened. The troubles and cares of this world introduced other issues and concerns into our life. Some were valid and some not, some real and some imagined. They represent ambient noise in our life. To be clear, I am well aware that some of this ambient noise may be absolutely necessary. It may be the "cost of doing business" of life. We have to pay the mortgage and the bills, and change the diapers. We cannot walk away from these things under the guise of finding the road less traveled. They are part of the journey.

The problem comes when the ambient noise of life starts to drown out the truer frequencies, the frequencies that capture our dreams, our hearts, and our visions for the future. Unfortunately, ambient noise is so pervasive, so omni-present, it never seems to stop, and usually increases rather than decreases over time. After a while we just stop looking for those frequencies that ring true in our heart and soul.

I believe this ambient noise in our life can be likened to the story of the seed that fell among the rocks in Jesus' parable of the Four Soils:

A farmer went out to plant some seed … Other seed fell among thorns that shot up and choked out the tender blades (Lk 8:5,7 NLT).

Jesus explained the parable by saying:

The seed is God's message … The thorny ground represents those who hear and accept the message, but all too quickly the message is crowded out by the cares and riches and pleasures of this life. And so they never grow into maturity (Lk 8:11,14 NLT).

The message that Jesus spoke of in the parable was the message of God to His children. It is interesting to note that this message – The Message! – was readily accepted by those who heard it. But so often the "cares and riches and pleasures of this life" come along and crowd the message out.

It is not so much the tragedies, monumental struggles, or life changing events and situations that Jesus talks about that overcome the message of God in our hearts. Rather, it is the ambient noise of life. It is the small, the mundane, the every day situations and events that force us off course. It is the incremental nature of the ambient noise, its accumulation over time, which magnifies our errors.

I am reminded of the statement "only those who take leisurely what the people of the world are busy about can be busy about what the people of the world take leisurely."[2] This statement reinforces the message in the parable of the Four Soils. Do we focus on what most of us are busy about – the cares, riches, and pleasures of this life – or the message of God? Jesus leaves us with little room to wonder about whether we can do both. He is clear in this parable when He says that one will choke out the other. We have only to choose which will be choked out.

Likewise, in our lives the ambient noise and those true frequencies that resonate in our soul cannot co-exist in harmony. At some point most of us decide to pay more attention to the ambient noise, though few of us realize this or verbalize the decision. Those things we cherished – those dreams, hopes, and aspirations – fade as we begin to take care of and focus on the day-to-day existence that seems appropriate at the time. This shift in focus on the present and away from our dreams moves us farther from our ideal self, the self we were created to be. So we drift along the path of mediocrity with so many others that the journey almost seems like the path on which we are supposed to be – almost.

But from time to time we get a glimpse of what can be. We

drop our guard. We dare to dream and come alive as we feel the energy that comes from a resurgence of hope in what lies before us. Then, like the sonar operator who has for too long watched only the graph of ambient noise, with its line after line of meaningless activity, we see something before us that moves us to act, but cannot be convinced that this is our time to grab the golden ring.

> *So the frequency we are looking for fades,*
> > *the ambient noise increases,*
> > > *and we return to just going through the motions.*
> *We withdraw to our cocoons.*

So, the first factor that derails us from our dreams of an abundant life is ambient noise. Although we will deal with solutions later, it is important that you develop a healthy awareness of the impact of ambient noise in your life.

What do you hear all day long? What is presented to your "sonar screen" of awareness? Does what you hear differ from what you would like to hear or see? How much perception is involved in the "reality" of the world as you see it? In Romans 12:2 (NIV) Paul said that we should not "conform any longer to the pattern of this world, but be transformed by the renewing of our mind." The world changes and our life is transformed when we change the way we think and the way we filter our reality – when we renew our mind. The world also changes when we do whatever it takes to master the ambient noise in our life so we might once again gain an awareness and appreciation for those frequencies that resonate within our soul.

PERSONAL REFLECTIONS

What did you used to dream about?

What kind of "ambient noise" caused you to give up on your dreams?

If the "ambient noise" were turned off and the truer frequencies were all that was left, what would you dream about now?

What would you like to spend your life pursuing?

LACK OF MODELING

I remember sitting through a psychology class in college and being captivated by a discussion on imprinting. Researchers found that ducklings and other animals "imprint" on their mother soon after birth. They bond with her and follow her everywhere.

Admittedly, there is nothing extraordinary about a duckling or anything else bonding with its mother. As a matter of fact, studies indicate that animals imprint on things other than their mother. They develop an intense attachment and sometimes try to emulate the behaviors of the objects they imprint upon. Interestingly enough, the criteria for being a model worthy of imprinting upon are really not that difficult to meet. Sometimes the object the newborns imprint upon is simply there – young seem to cling to whatever model is available. Sometimes the model is associated with food, comfort, or security to the newborn. Other times, the model they imprint upon is simply moving nearby and is adapted as something to follow. I am not an expert on imprinting or an authority on duck behavior, but I do wonder what would happen if there were more opportunities to "imprint" on appropriate models of abundant living.

Can you identify one person you have heard say, with passion and conviction, that he or she is doing exactly what God put him or her on the face of the earth to do? Have you heard people claim that they are, as the Blues Brothers claimed, "on a mission from God?" Do you know people who are so on fire that you know they are doing what God hard-wired them to do?

Usually, when I talk with people on this subject they struggle mightily and cannot even come up with one name. Try as they may, they just cannot seem to find the name of that individual who embodies the passion, commitment, joy, and Kingdom work that should be evident in someone who is living the abundant life and working directly for the King.

This inability to name role models represents a problem for you and me. As the ambient noise in our life increases, we try to juggle all of the balls that are thrown in our direction. College choice; degree choices; advanced degrees; marriage; children; friendships; social activities; civic clubs; upward mobility; church activities; career changes; politics in the career; physical and health changes; and so on.

We do pretty well at first. One ball in the air, then two, then three, then the big crash comes. We could juggle up to three, or thirty, or three hundred. The exact number is not important. What is important is that we all reach a point where there are too many balls in the air for us to handle. Your career is going fine but your son is in trouble or your wife is crying all of the time and she is starting to question if this is the way it will always be. All of a sudden the balls that you were juggling so comfortably before become unmanageable. As they start to fall, you react by picking them up and putting them back into the mix as quickly as possible, but they keep falling all over again.

The next thing we do is very similar to what my two-year-old does when he falls down. He looks up to see if Mommy and Daddy are close by. Even before he starts wailing he looks to see if the two people who help him define his little world are in the room. He wonders how they will react to this event in his life. So it is with us "big people" and the world we live in. We take our tumbles too, and get to the point where the ambient noise is drowning out everything else. In the midst of this we look around, hoping we will find someone who will help us make some sense of it all, someone who can validate the naïve, idealistic thoughts that run through our head.

Andy Stanley was speaking at a conference and humorously described my perspective during a period when I was really struggling at work. I had begun to wonder if there was something wrong with me. I felt like I was swimming against the current. I was constantly fighting battles and feeling lonely and bruised at the end of the day.

Stanley explained that such feelings are common among leaders. He went on to say: "You're not sick, you don't have a problem, you're a leader. God wired you that way." It was one of the most liberating moments of my entire life because it provided validation that I desperately needed. I needed someone to help make sense of my thoughts, my challenges, and the messages the world was sending me. I needed someone to tell me that I really was on the right path.

The problem is there are just too few of those people out there. We desperately need them to model the abundant life for us, because it is too easy to get caught up in the quagmire of every day existence. Without those people in our life we may give up on the quest for abundance.

Before I go further, I must clarify one thing. While there are people who may be regarded as role models, we must use some form of litmus test to determine if they really are role models of abundant living. One test I propose is an FFV test. FFV stands for Faith, Family, and Vocation. I believe role models who are genuine are well rounded and growing in all of these areas.

FFV forms the basic building blocks we need in order to have a well-balanced journey of our own. Many times in the corporate world we get so focused on vocation that faith and family get left by the wayside. Our role models are often people who are focused on vocation to the exclusion of everything else, which gives us the impression that is the way the world works. Role models such as these have little to contribute to the Faith and Family components of the life we are striving toward. Are they really worthy of being called role models?

I can remember with amazing clarity an encounter I had with a man who was at the top of a large organization. He wielded extreme power and authority over everyone within the organization. Although he was incredibly good at what he did, I was amazed to discover that he didn't really enjoy it. He did it because he was good at it. He did it out of duty. But it gave nothing substantive back to him. All it gave him was the hollow achievement of power, prestige, and money. All of which will one day be gone. I liked this man. I respected him. I was proud to work for him and his organization. But should he be my role model? Would abundance result from following the path he modeled?

Please understand. I am not deriding the need to strive for money, power, and position in a corporate environment, nor am I criticizing the need to achieve status, power, or wealth. That is where I have spent my adult life. In fact, it would be just as appropriate to discuss this topic with pastors who pour their life into their congregation's faith walk only to realize that they cannot sustain the pace. Oftentimes they suffer burn out because they do not achieve an adequate balance between work and family. They can also become so focused on their vocation – tending to and taking care of their church – that their own faith walk does not get the proper care.

We need people who are modeling the way life is supposed to be lived. We need people who will not sacrifice one area just to serve another. We need role models in significant positions of authority to encourage us to chase after our dreams, to live life to the fullest, to integrate Faith, Family and Vocation into an awesome abundance formula.

Jesus showed us the way. He said: "I have come that they may have life, and that they may have it more abundantly" (Jn 10:10). Anything less than abundant living – in any area of life – is simply not good enough. It is a direct contradiction to the message Jesus gave us 2,000 years ago.

Too often, we get the abundance sucked out of our life because we don't see enough people modeling it in their day-to-day existence. Too many people accept just getting by. We don't see enough people with the discipline, passion, and focus to live out the joy that Jesus wants us to have in our lives. Making the choice to live in such a manner is the only way we can begin to fill our lives with joy. We need models around us who exemplify the best in Faith, Family, and Vocation if we are going to let our joyful noise replace the ambient noises of mediocrity.

- Be around people who lift you, who propel you in the direction of your dreams.
- Pursue the abundant life incessantly.
- Find a genuine model.
- Model abundance for others.
- Become a Faith, Family, and Vocation advocate.
- Champion the abundant life.

PERSONAL REFLECTIONS

Have you imprinted on a lifestyle that is not fulfilling?

Who are some role models whose example of living in Faith, Family, and Vocation are worthy of study and emulation?

How can you spend more time around those people so that you see abundance modeled more often?

FEAR OF REJECTION

I sat down with Janice some time back and had a wonderful discussion about life, philosophy and faith. Janice and I interact frequently in our business dealings and in the civic club we both belong to. She is a very distinguished, hard working, industrious woman who is an absolute joy to talk with. As I learned more about her and her vision for life I became even more impressed with her.

One day she described an opportunity presented to her, but admitted that she feared she might not be able to live up to others' expectations. I said to Janice, "You know, none of us are quite as good as some people think we are." We openly discussed that we are all a little self-conscious and unsure of ourselves from time to time. Much of this uncertainty stems from the fact that we know our own weaknesses and failings better than anyone else possibly could. With this knowledge we become our own best, worst, and most consistent coach, friend, and ally.

Because of this we all suffer a bit of the "impostor syndrome." I worked with a consultant/trainer for a number of years whose wife was a psychologist. This unique family blend meant that I could always count on him to give a little off-handed insight into the human psyche. One of the most significant insights he ever gave me was his explanation of the "impostor syndrome." During his seminars, he taught us how to successfully "call" on and generate business with small business owners. He said that when we get ready to go on a call there is a little man, an impostor, sitting on our shoulder saying, "You're a fraud. They're going to find you out. You don't know what you're talking about. Everyone is going to know it pretty soon. Who are you trying to kid?"

When the impostor whispers to us, we think we are a fraud. We believe we are not who we say we are. We convince ourselves we have no business talking about this or that because we have failed in that area so many times before. We reason, what gives us the right to advise other people about a particular matter when we don't have it fixed in our own life yet?

These things go through our mind over and over as we strive for new heights and enter uncharted territory on the journey toward our potential. We get focused on things at work and all of our plans start coming together. Then a negative situation arises and the voice of our impostor whispers: "Look. You're not going to get it right consistently. Why even try?" The same thing happens at home as we break promises regarding the time and attention we would give to our spouse, our children, our finances, or whatever. In our faith walk, the Bible reading plan falls apart, we fall asleep during prayer, or we find ourselves thinking of things we committed to put out of our mind forever.

The simple fact is that all of the above relates directly or indirectly to a sense of rejection that we feel when we try and try and try but fail. When we don't meet our own expectations or keep our promises in our Faith, Family, and Vocation, we see it as not just a failure to do something, but an internal failure. Most of us will take that failure personally. We may see ourselves as the victim of circumstances and defend our failings vigorously to save face, but the fact is we internalize our failures and pre-empt the rejection of others by rejecting ourselves.

If we do this thing called life properly we are figuratively jumping up and down on the end of a limb as we shout gleefully at fulfilling our calling. "I have come that they may have life, and that they may have it more abundantly" (Jn 10:10). I'm going to say this as emphatically as I can. Abundance does not come from hugging trees. Sometimes you have to go out on a limb and occasionally that limb will give way beneath you. The occasional fall does not mean you are on the wrong path. Nor does it signal that you should hug the tree so tightly that all risk is avoided.

The good news is that as we grow accustomed to the limbs, we feel better and better about the life we are living. We gain confidence when we strive to actually do something with our life and effectively manage the associated risk. The bad news is that anytime we strive valiantly to accomplish anything of significance, there will always be obstacles and detractors waiting to "reject" us for what we are attempting to accomplish. The litany from naysayers usually sounds something like this:

"We have already tried that, it doesn't work."
"You can try it but don't get your hopes up."
"I really don't think that's the best way to go."
"Why are you doing this? Are you looking for a
    promotion?"
"Who are you trying to saddle up next to?"
"You know, that's just not the way we do things around
    here."

I am convinced that this chorus of negative responses, and others like them, do more damage to an abundance mentality than anything else. They cause us to start questioning ourselves, our motives, our dreams, everything. We start something with absolute purity of motives, enthusiastic about the difference we can make, and are greeted at the door by cynicism and negativity. Immediately we are taken aback and more than a little offended. We resent the hurtful criticism and we feel the anger swell up in us.

So we begin doubting ourselves and start giving a little less each day. We don't rock the boat like we did before because that's not the way things are done or that's not the "proper" way to get things done. We lose our focus on the elements of Faith, Family, and Vocation, believing we must conform to other people's expectations or we simply fail to take the necessary risks that lead to achieving the abundance that Jesus promised we can have.

Unfortunately, too many of us discount that promise. When forced to choose between abundance and conformity we say things like: "As a young lawyer I have to stay until 8 p.m. each night. That's just the way it's done." Translation? I know I am not living as I should. My career may thrive but my wife and child will pay the price, and will eventually get used to my not being a part of their life. It's not worth the price that I will have to pay, but I don't have the courage to step out of line and do what I know I should. I will be rejected if I try to live differently.

"Everyone gossips. That's just the way things are there." Translation? I know gossip serves no positive purpose and that it is an enemy to peace and harmony in relationships. I could easily say that I'm just not comfortable talking about other people, but I decide not to honor that because I fear rejection. I could be the subject of their next conversation. I feel guilty, but I feel worse about possibly being rejected by such little people.

Fear of rejection immobilizes us throughout our life. We learn to play within the narrow parameters of the status quo so that those around us will accept us. But we get so restricted by these parameters that we lose the ability to truly impact our world. We evolve into a state similar to that described by C.S. Lewis: "We make men without chests and expect of them virtue and enterprise. We laugh at honor and are shocked to find traitors in our midst. We castrate and then bid the geldings to be fruitful."[3]

We cannot have it both ways. We cannot allow the fear of rejection to haunt our steps, to keep us from being what we were created to be, and expect our life to be any different. Sometimes we will be rejected when we live ethically and morally. Sometimes we will be rejected when we insist on abundance in all areas of our life – Faith, Family, and Vocation.

But in the midst of the pain of rejection, a new depth can be carved out within us. A depth that says we are willing to go to any lengths to do what God put in our heart to do. Winston Churchill said, "Success is going from failure to failure without a loss of enthusiasm." A mentor of mine amplified Churchill's advice when he told me years ago, "Never let anyone make you feel like you have to apologize for doing your job to the best of your ability." Both of these gentlemen are right. Don't let failures, rejection or criticism keep you from striving for the abundant life. When we try repeatedly to stretch the parameters that define our life, despite failure and rejection, we are on the right track.

So many people get caught up in the fear of rejection. They hear the chorus of conformity to worldly standards that only lead to brokenness and fail to listen to that voice crying out within them to do something with their life. No one can discern for you what God has put in your heart to do. Listen to people. Seek wise counsel, but pay attention to that small voice within. It is this voice that allowed Peter to deal with fear of rejection when he faced the Sanhedrin for preaching the name of Jesus. After being jailed for a night and facing their inquisition, Peter must have felt the anger and resentment that comes from someone rejecting or denying your most basic beliefs.

So many of us stop going full throttle with our beliefs because we don't want to deal with rejection or criticism. Peter dealt with it differently. Acts 4:18 (NIV) records that the Sanhedrin "called them in again and commanded them not to speak or teach at all in the name of Jesus." This edict meant that Peter had been thoroughly censored. Instead of retreating, spending time to challenge their beliefs, or seeking alternative courses of action, Peter made a simple statement. "Judge for yourselves whether it is right in God's sight to obey you rather than God. For we cannot help speaking about what we have seen and heard" (Acts 4:19 NIV).

Don't be a lone wolf.
   Do be prayerful.
      Do be judicious.
         Don't be stupid.

But don't fear the inevitable rejection. The only way to avoid it is to fly so far under the radar that you will be undetected – guaranteed to have little impact on the world.

We'll talk more about this in upcoming chapters, but please bookmark the words of Peter: "For we cannot help speaking about what we have seen and heard." God has wired you a certain way and He speaks to you a certain way. God put something in your heart that is not in your neighbor's heart. Take counsel with God and listen closely for His guidance, but be more selective about the guidance that you accept from the rest of the world. Don't let rejection thwart you from your God-ordained journey to abundance.

PERSONAL REFLECTIONS

Identify an instance when you have been rejected for trying to do the right thing.

Examine an instance when you have been rejected for trying to do something extraordinary – something outside the normal bounds of the hordes of mediocrity. Record your thoughts.

Think of an instance when people with small or no vision caused you to put the right vision, the right plan, maybe even a God-inspired plan on hold. Describe it here:

Think of those people who have rejected you because you have tried to stretch to greater heights. Did they cause you to change course; back down; give up? Describe how you handled the criticism.

How has fear of rejection affected your commitment toward your dream or living the life you should?

FEAR IN GENERAL

I go to leadership conferences every year, with two of my favorites being the Willow Creek Leadership Summit and INJOY's Catalyst Conference. The common element with these conferences is that they are both centered on Christian leadership with particular guidance and emphasis to pastors of local churches. An unspoken theme in these conferences is to recognize and confront the fear that dwells within each of us.

Pastor, you have a member of your church, a heavy contributor, who is destructive in his influence in certain areas. Do you confront him? Do you deal with the issue up front or do you just ignore it, because you need his tithe and the tithe of his wealthy friends?

Sales Manager, you constantly preach "teamwork." You believe that when everyone contributes to the group, then the group as a whole benefits with increased sales and camaraderie. But your top salesperson is an avowed "lone wolf." He never shares ideas or best practices and is close-lipped when asked for help by his peers.

What would you do in either of these situations? Would you push the issue and require more? Would you risk losing your top sales performer for the good of the group or will you wait until performance and morale decreases in the entire team before you deal with the issue? Do you find yourself looking the other way because you don't want to upset a wealthy tither?

Was there a time when you would not have hesitated to confront the "lone wolf?" Where has your idealism gone? Where did the person go who put the good of the church first? What are you afraid of? How did fear creep its way into your ability to manage, to lead, to live your life to the fullest?

Fred or John or Tracy or Sue – whatever your name might be. You have made it to a point in your career or life where you have found contentment. You or someone in your family makes enough money for you to be comfortable with your life. But deep inside you know there is something missing. Deep inside you feel you may actually die if you are forced to live this way forever. You know you are not wired to do what you are doing right now. You like your job and are thankful for it but know that it is not your dream. You are not being unrealistic in what you can accomplish, but you know that you have missed your calling.

Will *you* answer? Your job pays the bills, and you enjoy it most of the time. It will feed the family, but it will not feed the hunger deep inside of you. What will you do? Will you walk from security for the sake of a dream? Will you be satisfied with a cabin in the valley when the mansion on the hill awaits? What would people think? Do you think you can honor your faith, family and vocational walk with the life you are now living?

Have you ever looked at people who were living the life that you are now, and secretly prayed you would never do that? What would your assessment be of your current life? Do your dreams bring energy or sadness? Do you even dream anymore? What has happened to your idealism? What keeps you from stepping out on the limb? Could it be the fear of falling? Could it be the fear of failing? Could it be that the dual drugs of comfort and security have deadened your senses to fulfilling your life's destiny? Do you scoff at the notion of even having a life destiny? What are you afraid of? How has fear crept its way into your career decisions, your striving, and your life?

Fred, John, Tracy, or Sue. You get so many facets of your life in order and feel good about your existence. But then children come along and a deep awakening stirs within you. You realize that you need more of a faith walk in your life. You enjoy going to church again. Your faith gets stronger and you do most of the "right" things. Prayer before each meal is a given with you and your family as long as you are at home, at church, or with another church family. But in public you feel so self-conscious that you cannot bring yourself to do it consistently, and it bothers you.

You don't feel like you're being honest in your relationship with God. You feel the urge to tell people who are simply going through the motions what your relationship with Jesus has

Living the Abundant Life

done for you. You want to tell them there is another way, that life does not have to be meaningless. You want to assure them that you have changed through His help and that they have the same power available.

You want to tell people what is on your heart. But you don't say anything. You keep your relationships superficial and go your own separate way, but deep inside you're dying because you know that you are being called to share your faith. You feel led to share the Good News and you want to so very badly. But you just can't bring yourself to do it.

Why is it that difficult? What is it that puts the barrier up? What are you afraid of? How did fear creep its way into your social interactions, your friendships, your responding to the Great Commission? When did fear start superseding God? How did He take a backseat?

It is fear that prevents you from becoming what you have been wired by God to be. It is fear that prevents you from giving your best. Are you afraid of what others will say? Are you afraid that your family, who knows you best, will think you're a fraud when you try to walk openly as a Godly believer? Are you afraid that if you say to your friends "I don't do that anymore" they will laugh at you, question your motives, or reject you? Are you afraid you will fail or look stupid? Do you believe you should be content with what you have? Are you afraid that what you have is all that you will ever have?

This is not a pretty picture – nor is it intended to be. If we are going to have "life more abundantly" then we have to be committed to a life that is constantly in open warfare against fear. One of my personal commitments is to "resist and confront fear of anything as if it is trying to take away my very next breath." Paul counseled Timothy on the subject when he wrote: "For God has not given us a spirit of fear, but of power and of love and of a sound mind" (2 Tim 1:7). If God did not give me a spirit of fear, then any time I am confronted or weighed down by it I must consider its source. If it is not of God, then I must resist it as if it is trying to take away my next breath.

Chuck Swindoll wrote that the most often repeated

command from the mouth of Jesus was to "fear not."[4] We see over and over that fear has a constant, often debilitating effect on our life. If the above examples strike a familiar chord, let me encourage you to begin working through any fear that stands between you and abundance in your faith, family, and vocation.

Fear does not have a place in the decision making process of the man or woman seeking to live a Godly life. Caution is good. Being prudent is great. But fear leads to paralysis and cuts us off from all of those good things that contribute to our abundance.

As we close this section on fear, take a few moments to be honest about the impact of fear in your life. We all have to deal with it from time to time. The specifics of fear are particular to each of us based on our experiences, circumstances, thought patterns, and so on. Spend some quality time on the following Personal Reflections.

PERSONAL REFLECTIONS

What are some things that you would like to do but have not, because you let fear stop you?

What are some of the things that you used to dream about, but let fear over something dissolve your dream?

Living the Abundant Life

What is your greatest fear?

What has God called you to do that you have not done? What are you afraid of?

EXHAUSTION

As we get closer to the end of the discussion on those things that rob us of the search for an abundant life, it is essential that we deal with the obvious. We have looked at ambient noise, the lack of role models to show us the way, the fear of rejection, and fear in general. Hopefully all of these make some sense when we look at how we lose our way. But the pace of modern life leads to one of the biggest reasons that we give up on the abundant life. Quite simply, we are tired. We are worn out by the pace of life. We spend so much time juggling so many balls that we become numb to the experience. Let me give an example.

You go to work for 10-12 hours a day, Monday through Friday. Every week or so you have a dinner or another function to attend in the evening. You may do church or a small group one night a week. Soccer season starts and it's Tuesday for one child and Thursday for another. You want to get your Master's degree and feel it's necessary to "punch the ticket," so you chip away at that once a week and do plenty of reading in between. You take work home each day, too. Your spouse has "girls night out" or a "night out with the boys" periodically and you want to support that.

Does this sound busy? We haven't even made it to the weekend! Soccer practice takes up three hours between the two children on Saturday morning so there's no sleeping in. The baby turns into something inhuman if she doesn't get a nap at noon, so you always plan to be around the house at that time. The grass takes an hour to cut or maintain, so you have to schedule that for after the little one settles into her nap. Then you have about 30 minutes of free time before you start cleaning the house for the dinner guests who will arrive at 6 o'clock. They come over and you have a wonderful time. They leave at around 9:30 p.m., then you spend another hour cleaning up. After a few minutes talking about the visit and watching the news, you realize how absolutely exhausted you are. You collapse into bed and fall into the deepest sleep you can remember.

On Sunday morning you realize you have slept a little longer than intended. You get out of bed, get the coffee going, retrieve the paper, and have 15 minutes of "free time" before waking up the children. You start getting them ready for church and everything goes pretty well until 30 minutes prior to time to leave. Then it hits you that you're behind. The tension escalates and your voice takes on the tone of a dictator barking orders to dissidents. You rush into church 10 minutes late and are totally unprepared for the development of your faith walk! One lady I know commented "I lost my religion for 30 years trying to get my children ready for church on Sunday morning!" Sound familiar?

The question I want you to consider is this: Can you sustain this pace? Can you keep going through the motions like the ones described above and have any sanity left at the end of the day?

We have evolved into beings who can sleepwalk through the day and actually make it look normal. We feel odd when we get a few hours to do nothing. Sometimes we even feel a little guilty about it. We cannot keep doing this. We are running on fumes.

The exhaustion comes from the fact that we know we can't

do it all, and yet we desperately keep trying. We want our children to be involved in everything and we drive ourselves insane to provide those opportunities. We consider every group of people a networking opportunity and wear ourselves out painting on the smile and pouring down the coffee long enough to pass out a card or two. We say "yes" to everything we're asked to do whether we're good at it or not, because we like being wanted and feel like we should.

Please hear this message loud and clear. I know you need to generate business. I know you want your children to have it better than you did. I know that serving your church gives you a sense of satisfaction. But I also suspect that you spend considerable time in a zombie-like state from all of this activity. I spoke with an ultra-successful executive recently who admitted she would get bored if she had a week off to do nothing. Her fatigue was evident though, as she lamented that for once in her life she would like to try boredom.

See if this sounds familiar: You do so much for your children that you are exhausted when you are with them, and they don't get enough of what they need the most – you! You attend the dinners because you feel you should, but leave feeling dissatisfied because you know you are cheating your family by working so late. Pretty soon you start resenting the dinners, and neglect to give your clients or potential clients your full time and attention. You dutifully attend church activities, but they just become another perfunctory date on your calendar. You earn a reputation for your selfless service to your church, but deep down inside you know that your service has just become another job and your faith walk isn't as satisfying as it used to be. Amidst this frantic pace of activities your church, your children, your clients, and God are all asking for the same thing – you. But they don't want what you are currently offering – a person so frazzled that the best you have to offer never has time to be seen. They want the REAL YOU, not a counterfeit.

Bill Hybels, pastor to over 20,000 people at Willow Creek church and an international leader in church growth and leadership, wrote the following in his incredible article entitled

The Art of Self-Leadership:[5]

Is my pace sustainable? I came close to a total emotional meltdown in the early 1990s. Suffice it to say I didn't understand self-leadership. I didn't understand the principle of sustainability. I fried my emotions. I abused my spiritual gifts. I damaged my body. I neglected my family and friends. And I came within a whisker of becoming a statistic.

I remember sitting in a restaurant and writing: 'The pace at which I've been doing the work of God is destroying God's work in me.' Then I remember putting my head down on my spiral notebook in that restaurant and sobbing.

But I asked myself, 'Bill, who has a gun to your head? Who's forcing you to bite off more than you can chew? Who's intimidating you into over-committing? Whose approval and affirmation and applause other than God's are you searching for that makes you live this way?' The answers were worse than sobering. They were devastating.

The elders, to whom I'm accountable, did not cause my pace problem. It wasn't caused by the board, staff, family, or friends. The whole pace issue was a problem of my own making. I had no one else to blame. That's a terribly lonely feeling – having no one else to blame.

So I sat all alone in this cheap restaurant in South Haven, mad as a hornet that I couldn't blame anybody for my kingdom exhaustion and my emotional numbness. To find the bad guy, I had to look in a mirror.

To further complicate matters, the only person who can put a sustainability program together for your future is you. For 15 years, I lived overcommitted and out of control, and deep down I kept saying, 'Why aren't the elders rescuing me? Why aren't my friends rescuing me? Don't people see I'm dying here?'

But it wasn't their job. It's my job. Please, if you haven't already, commit yourself to developing an approach to leadership that will enable you to endure over the long haul.

Bill Hybels is an exceptional leader and a man who has been remarkably gifted by God for what he is doing. Yet he cannot do it all himself and openly admits that he almost became a statistic, because he "didn't understand the principle of sustainability."

You can't do it all either – and you shouldn't try! What you need, what you must have in order to have an abundant life, is a fully charged, energized you. Take a look at the way you have been living your life and ask yourself if your children, your spouse, your job, your church, is getting the real you or a counterfeit. Then take a step back and determine how you can schedule your time so you can meet your responsibilities and recharge your batteries.

You may feel selfish when you insist on your own personal time. But you must realize that you cannot give the world your best unless you schedule adequate time for rest, relaxation, contemplation, and growth. A fully energized you can live the abundant life and pour out that abundance upon others.

If you have ever felt exhausted mentally and physically, welcome to the club. We all struggle with too much work and too many "top" priorities. The good news is that you can set a nd maintain *your* priorities, and that abundance begins with establishing those priorities in your faith, family, and vocation walks.

Let me emphasize again that you can't do it all and you shouldn't feel like you have to or should. We will delve deeper into this later but start working on this mindset now. You are wired to do some pretty amazing things and you should do them. In your faith, family, and vocation you should probably carve out more time in your schedule for those things that you are wired by God to be strong at. Conversely, there are so many things that we find ourselves committed to that add little to the Kingdom or to living abundantly in faith, family, and vocation. Frequently we swim against the current when we load our calendars with concerns that add little value and that do not play to our strengths – particularly those strengths given to us by God.

Add to your calendar those fulfilling activities that will make your life count. In all areas of life build strengths into your schedule and start leveraging what God has given you to build the life you should have. As you do this you will, by necessity, remove things that do not add to the life you desire. The pace of life will always dictate that something be pushed off our calendar or priority list. Ensure that those things that are pushed aside are the lowest priorities that add the least to your life. We will never regret their being displaced by the really important things in life. These are the priorities that you, and only you, can and must set.

If you want to live abundantly, you will have to take some time to rest, to put up your feet and relax, to just sit around and enjoy the act of breathing. You must recharge your batteries and honor your priorities. If you neglect who you are and what you are supposed to be, you will be of no use to yourself, your dreams, or anyone else. So prioritize your way toward incredible abundance.

PERSONAL REFLECTIONS

Do you frequently find yourself mentally and physically exhausted? Why?

Do your highest life priorities make it on your calendar first? Why not?

Do the lowest priorities and "brushfires" occupy much of your time and mental energy? Why?

What do you need to let go of or say "no" to?

What do you need to put so high on the priority list that nothing can take its place?

SETTLING

We have reviewed a number of factors that cause us to get off track. These things cause us to give up the search for abundance for one reason or another. When faced with fear of rejection we may simply "settle" into a mode of behavior where we are no longer open to such rejection. When there is so much ambient noise out there, we may get confused in the search for significance and abundance and "settle for less" by deciding to forego the hunt altogether. The noise doesn't seem so bad when you're not fighting against it. Without role models, we may "settle" into self-defeating behavioral patterns that can cut off our abundance at the knees.

C.S. Lewis wrote, "We are half-hearted creatures, fooling around with drink and sex and ambition, when infinite joy is offered us. Like an ignorant child who wants to go on making mud pies in a slum because he cannot imagine what is meant by an offer of a holiday at the sea, we are far too easily pleased."[6]

At the end of the day, when all factors are considered, one thing remains: We must choose whether or not to strive for abundance, to get to the marrow of life, or to settle for something else. I have heard it said that the "good in life is the enemy of the best in life." This epitomizes what it means to settle for less. We get to the point where things are going okay, and we stop right there. We push and push until we get momentum moving in the right direction and then we pull back.

Far too often we stop pushing, not so much from the consequences of a fall from grace, but because we have "arrived." We pull back because we think that making better "mud pies" means we have really achieved something. We can't imagine that there really is a sea of abundance out there.

We settle for less. We pull away. We disengage from the very things that keep the fire lit within us. And as the fire becomes an ember, we take stock of what is left and thank our lucky stars that we didn't take risks because we recognized when enough is enough. "You can't live in a dream world forever" would be a coy way of describing and justifying our mediocre choices.

When you think about such a rational way of going about life, it certainly doesn't inspire thoughts of grandeur, does it? But then again, it also might not strike you as a horrible or sinful way to live. That being the case, consider the following example that Jesus gives in the Story of the Ten Servants in Luke 19 (NLT):

> *A nobleman was called away to a distant empire to be crowned king and then return. Before he left, he called together ten servants and gave them ten pounds of silver to invest for him ... When he returned, the king called in the servants to whom he had given the money. He wanted to find out what they had done with the money and what their profits were. The first servant reported a tremendous gain – ten times as much as the original amount. "Well done!" the king exclaimed. "You are a trustworthy servant. You have been faithful with the little I entrusted to you, so you will be governor of ten cities as your reward."*
>
> *The next servant also reported a good gain ... "Well done!" the king said. "You can be governor over five cities."*
>
> *But the third servant brought back only the original amount of money and said, "I hid it and kept it safe. I was afraid because you are a hard man to deal with, taking what isn't yours and harvesting crops you didn't plant."*
>
> *"You wicked servant!" the king roared. "Hard, am I? If you knew so much about me and how tough I am, why didn't you deposit the money in the bank so I could at least get some interest on it?"*

The first two servants received rewards commensurate with the work they did for the king. The last servant was reprimanded by the king for his efforts. What did he do to deserve such a beating? The servant did not abuse what was given to him. He seemed mindful, even fearful, of the king and of displeasing him. What the servant did was nothing. He hid the money, then presented it safe and sound upon the king's return.

Nothing in the Bible is there by coincidence, so we are left to ponder the significance of this story. Why did Jesus tell it? What does it mean to us? I believe it directly addresses the issue of settling.

The last servant settled. He took what he was given and made the decision to do nothing because of immobilizing fear. Jesus, through this story, says to us that this approach to life is unacceptable. Each of us has been given certain gifts, and are expected to use them. In fact, if we are going to live the abundant life and please the King it is absolutely necessary that we use our gifts. We must put to use what God has given us.

Why do we settle? Why do we fail to use our gifts for the Kingdom-work that is waiting to be done? I was enlightened on this point by my good friend and Pastor Bryan Collier. Bryan pointed out that "we settle because we believe our gifts are given for our use and our standards are met with so little effort." Our standards are simply not high enough to fully employ the gifts God has given us. Our loftiest goals are only consolation prizes if we miss the honor of working for God using the gifts He gave us for the task. Another reason we settle for less is our schedules are so full that we have no time for Kingdom-work. There is no time for pursuing a dream that doesn't seem feasible anyway.

Think about this. Let us say that the king gave the first servant some silver to invest. Upon returning to his country, the king inquired about the silver and the servant replied that he hadn't gotten around to investing it yet. He had some other investments he had to take care of before dealing with the king's concerns. Can you imagine what the king's response would have been? What do you suppose would happen to such a negligent servant?

Yet that is the answer so many of us give each day. We go about our day-to-day activities and for one reason or another settle into a routine where we are not striving for the abundant life. Good enough has become – well, good enough. We don't think there's anything wrong with it. It might even be a sign of maturity, but waiting in the wings is the King who will one day ask what we have done with what He has given us to invest. Will we respond that we didn't have time? Will we say we were unclear about what He wanted us to do, so we chose to do nothing? How would we expect *our* King to react to such statements?

You and I are hard-wired to make an impact in this world and specifically gifted by God for our role. But we often settle for less and it is such a shame. To quote C.S. Lewis again: "We are far too easily pleased." Tommy Newberry wrote that we can "walk up to the ocean of abundance with either a thimble or a tanker truck."[7] The choice is completely our own. Thimble or tanker truck, striving or settling, abundance or good enough. Which will it be? The choice is ours.

PERSONAL REFLECTIONS

Are you carrying out your unique role today?

Is your relationship with God what you want it to be? Elaborate.

Are you the mother, father, husband, wife, or friend that you want to be? Elaborate.

If Jesus physically accompanied you to work for the next week, would you be proud of the routine He would see? Elaborate.

Are you living life to the fullest or settling for less?

"Who am I?" The question hides within the recesses of our soul, but surfaces in subtle ways as we constantly look forward to tomorrow, hoping that it will offer more fulfillment than today. We dabble in drink or drug, investments or politics, gossip or self-help. We choose anything that takes our mind off the fact that today is so boring we cannot imagine many more tomorrows just like this. Or, we allow the minutiae to overload our lives so completely that we cannot imagine the level of abundance we could enjoy if we honored our calling.

We pay so much attention to ambient noise that we couldn't hear the guidance and counsel of our ideal self if it screamed in our ear.

We might push harder to become everything our soul tells us we should be, but it's too hard to find encouragement in the form of credible role models. It can be intimidating to travel on this journey and there seems to be no one who will come alongside and say, "I've been on this road before. You may get beat up, sometimes badly, but you're on the right path. And though I can't always help you in those battles, I'll be right here with you. You will never walk alone." We do not have enough of these people in our life.

We sleepwalk through our days in such an exhausted condition that we cannot even imagine what might await us. We are overloaded with tasks and priorities, and the battles of the past still weigh heavily on our minds. Our baggage gets heavier and heavier. Instead of dragging it around with us, we decide to set up camp right where we are.

So we bargain with life. We make a deal that we will not push, will not strive, and will not stay out on the edge of the limb if life will stop dealing with us so roughly. We settle for an existence that provides some cognitive stimulation but rarely links that cognition with our soul. We desperately want more out of life and cannot imagine why abundance has not dropped on our doorstep. And we imagine that everything would be all right if we could have daily doses of abundance.

All the while we forget that we are the ones who limit our abundance. We are the ones who decide if life is too difficult. At some point we decide that we are no longer willing to pay the price. We just want to relax.

We grow tired of being attacked every time we make a decision. We resent people taking shots at us. We grow tired of doing great things, only to fall down the next day. We get irritated at hearing lame advice from people who have never experienced what we want to experience, yet seem to think they are experts at critiquing our journey.

So we stop searching for the abundant life that Jesus promised we might have. But we don't stop wondering or wandering. And try as we may we cannot get rid of that deep gnawing within us that cries out, "This is not all that I'm here for." In his insightful book, *The Journey of Desire*, John Eldredge describes that gnawing within. He says:

> By the grace of God, we cannot quite pull it off. In the quiet moments of the day we sense a nagging within, a discontent, a hunger for something else. But because we have not solved the riddle of our existence, we assume that something is wrong – not with life, but with us.[8]

Having the hunger, having the discontent, means all is not lost. There is nothing wrong with us – we just "have not solved the riddle of our existence." It is to this riddle that we now turn.

Do you still embrace your dreams, your hopes, your visions, your life with as much enthusiasm as before? If not, why?

Do you believe that you can have an incredible life? Why or why not?

This chapter lists six factors that get you off course in your quest for abundance: Ambient noise, lack of modeling, fear of rejection, fear in general, exhaustion, and settling. Which two or three factors have had or are having the biggest negative effect on your quest for abundance?

How did each factor get you off course?

In John 10:10, Jesus says, "I have come that they may have life, and that they may have it more abundantly." We know we have a problem. We know He came that we might have an abundant life but that life is often not what we experience. Before we can live an abundant life, we have to answer the same question the man at the pool of Bethesda had to answer. John 5:5-6 (NLT) records: *One of the men lying there had been sick for thirty-eight years. When Jesus saw him and knew how long he had been ill, he asked him, "Would you like to get well?"*

We will not always be immediately healed when we answer that question in the affirmative. But we will not get better or have abundance until we determine that we want to get well. Do you want to get well?

Do you want to live an abundant life?

What will you do today to improve your life in the realms of faith, family and vocation?

2

WHAT IS THE ALTERNATIVE?

Until now the focus has been on why we are not living as we should. The emphasis has been on the difficulties, the problems, those things that keep us from truly getting the most out of life – from living an abundant life.

Ambient noise drowns out the strong signals of that great life that lies before us. Lack of modeling keeps us from recognizing that there is a different way to live. Fear of rejection makes us step away from success though it may be right in front of us. Fear also causes us to retreat to the deceptive comfort of a false protective shell. We fail to risk striving for abundance and end up dying inside. Exhaustion makes us believe we cannot go any further, no matter how much abundance awaits us. Settling for less convinces us that less is enough. Meanwhile, that something within us that makes us special and holds the key to our greatness slowly dies.

This chapter represents a shift in direction. We have previously looked at the problem; now we will focus on the alternative. And that solution may be less complex than you might suspect. The crux of this chapter is John 10:10. It is the main point of this book and should be a central theme of our lives. In that verse Jesus said, "I have come that they may have life, and that they may have it more abundantly." The answer to the problems and woes that keep us from being who and what we are supposed to be is the abundant life that He spoke of. After all, if Jesus said that He came so that we could "have life AND have it more abundantly," doesn't that suggest that He wants us to have both?

In the chapters which follow, I will go into more detail about what abundant living looks like. For now though, I want to define a key element of abundant living. Abundant living is living so that at the end of your life you will be able to look at your efforts and say, "For this I came." Abundant living is doing what you came to do each and every day. It is mastering your focus on and balance between your faith, family and vocation.

Abundant living is about being the same person all day, every day. Think of each of the three essential components of your life – Faith, Family, and Vocation. For each of these parts choose someone who knows you well. For instance, you may want to choose a friend who is in your small group at church and with whom you share your spiritual struggles and victories. Your spouse might be your choice for the family representative. A confidante at work could represent the vocational arena of your life.

Take a moment and write down the answers to the following questions. You can answer these in several different ways. You might consider how each of these people would answer the same questions. Or, if you really want to venture out, you might ask these people the questions and use the space below to document their responses.

PERSONAL REFLECTIONS

How would the person who is closest to you in your faith walk answer the following questions about you?

Who are you?

What is important to you?

What do you care about the most?

How would the person who knows your family life and relationships answer the following about you?

Who are you?

What is important to you?

What do you care about the most?

How would the person who knows you best in your vocation answer the following about you?

Who are you?

What is important to you?

What do you care about the most?

The first answer you might get will probably be your work title or role – what you do. But what we are looking to find is not what you do, but who and what you are. Once you've gotten all of the responses to the Faith, Family, and Vocational arenas of your life, compile them and then answer the following questions: How similar are the answers? Do they all say the same thing? Does the person at church describe you in the same manner as the person at work? Does your family describe you in the same way as those at work? How consistent are their assessments?

Many times people report that there is a great deal of difference between the descriptions they receive. In particular, the description at work differs significantly from the description at home or church. For example, a friend of mine told me about the time his wife shared with him the incredible things his employees had to say about him. This is a man whose enthusiasm and passion for people are truly phenomenal. He is the ultimate leader and people would gladly walk through fire for him. After hearing his flock of admirers sing his praises, his wife finally made her request. She said, "You know that man they tell me about, the one I hear all of the stories about? I want *that* man. I want *that* man in our home and with our children."

Bear in mind that her husband is no average man. He has been and continues to be a great role model for me. At the time of that dramatic conversation with his wife, he could not possibly have loved his family any more. He was and is consumed by them. But that statement by his wife brought him face-to-face with the reality that who he was depended on where he was and what he was doing.

Why the difference? It would be easy to say that we are required to do different things at work than we are at home or in our faith walk. But it's not that easy. The answer goes much deeper. We often feel compelled to be someone else depending on which area of life we are operating in at the moment.

We get up on Monday morning and realize that we have to change "the mask" we have been wearing over the weekend. So we put on our work mask, don our work personality, and head toward the office. We walk around all day in our work mask and we act the part because that is how we are expected to behave.

Then, as soon as we clock out we have to get in our car, change our mask, and head off to wherever we are going. Going home? We need to put the "Dad" or "Mom" mask on – patient, kind, in-charge, whatever the parent personality dictates. Going to church? We need to put our "wise, humble and spiritual" mask on. Pretty soon we start getting our masks confused. We have no clue who we are or if we are wearing a mask at all. We forget what we really look like.

The impact of this can be devastating. If you have to change your personality every time you step into your Faith, Family, or Vocation roles, you are putting yourself into a multiple personalities dilemma. It is extremely difficult to create separate characters to play in the different roles of life: one character for Faith, one for Family, and another for Vocation. If your intent is to compartmentalize the roles, you will lose yourself in the process. You will end up in a condition I call spiritual schizophrenia.

Your schizophrenia, your separation from reality, is a spiritual one in that you are denying nothing less than how God made you. You were created by God in His image to be one person and to do all things for His glory based on the unique form of His image that you bear. When you try to separate that image into little parts depending on where you are and what you are doing, you are separating yourself from reality. God wants you all in one piece. He has created you to walk on your own unique path toward the abundance He has in store for you.

First and foremost living the abundant life means having consistency between the different elements of your life. You cannot live the abundant life if there is constant war being waged between Faith, Family, and Vocation. There must be consistency between the elements and they must be complimentary, in some form, so that you are not just enduring each of the three roles, but embracing them as gifts from God. You cannot "endure" your way into abundance.

You must live in constant search for abundance, and that search must include your Faith, Family, and Vocation as intertwined and complimentary elements of life. Living in this manner will enable you to walk freely in the different areas of life by integrating each of the three roles so you can be who you truly are within each. In doing this you drop the masks because you won't need them anymore. There will be consistency between what you are doing and who you are.

ABUNDANCE IS MASK-FREE LIVING.

Refer back to our earlier exercise and allow me to pose one more question. We looked at what others would say about you and considered what the differences in their answers meant. Now, take a moment and consider what you would like each of them to say about you.

PERSONAL REFLECTIONS

What would you like your pastor or your closest spiritual friend to say about you?

What would you like your children to say about you?

Living the Abundant Life

What would you like your husband or wife to say about you?

What would you like your co-workers to say about you?

Remember, we're not looking for superficial answers here. Ignore the easy answers and get to the heart of the matter. What would you *really* like them to say about you? What are the common values and attributes that you would like to see reflected in your life?

Compare the answers from both exercises. Compare what you thought they would say to what you would like them to say. Are there differences? What does that tell you? If there are big differences between these two assessments, are you wearing multiple masks? What mask do you wear the most? The least? Which mask feels most comfortable for you?

No matter what you do or how well you do it you will not live an abundant life unless there is a complimentary relationship between all of the different areas of your life. When you stop interchanging the masks and start living based on who you are and what you were made to be, you will begin to move fearlessly toward the ideal self that God made you to be. Striving for this ideal self is extremely important. As you try to figure out why you came, why you are here, you must also determine where you want to go with that knowledge and for whom you will serve.

The ideal self represents the person God made you to be right now and the person He wants you to be 10, 20, or 30 years from now. It is essential for you to consider who you are and who you will be. It is absolutely necessary for you to make a decision about what you are going to do, who you are going to be, and how you are going to live your life. So as you start working through your own search for abundance you must consider who it is that you are to be at the end of the journey. It is a journey that is wrought with peril and disappointment, but it is well worth the price.

God wants each of us to live abundant lives. He wants it so badly that Jesus came to personally deliver and oversee the distribution of abundance to those who would accept and live it out in faith. Jesus said "I am the way and the truth and the life" (Jn 14:6 NLT) and His command to the disciples is the same command He issues to us now: "Follow me."

"Follow me," He says, and Zaccheus climbs down from the tree, repents, and changes his entire lifestyle.

"Follow me," He says, and the disciples put down their nets and leave their business endeavors.

"Follow me," He says, and a small band of believers transforms the world forever.

He is still saying, "Follow me," when He says that He came so that we would "have life and have it more abundantly." I propose that if you are not striving for abundance, seeking that state where joy overflows, thinking about it every day, then you may need to turn your eyes again to the One who calls to you. Agreeing to His invitation to follow means more than accepting His love, His gifts, and His redemption. It also means accepting His purpose and demonstrating that purpose in your life.

Consider this. If you don't accept the salvation that comes from the cross, you are rejecting the greatest gift of Jesus and thereby rejecting Him! That doesn't make sense to someone who claims to be a Christ follower. We wouldn't dream of doing that. Likewise, if you don't accept and pursue the abundance that He said He came to provide ... well, that just doesn't make sense coming from someone who claims to be a Christ follower. Abundance is not a way of living but the way of living if we are really following Jesus.

Living the abundant life is more than receiving gifts and being blessed. Life dictates that we will have up and down periods, and we must take the good with the bad. Abundant living means that we take the good with the bad and live abundantly anyway. We recognize that neither we nor the world is perfect, but we can choose to live an abundant life. We can elect to let our joy spill over and find the good in each day. We can find purpose and achieve significance each day.

ABUNDANCE IS DETERMINING THAT THE ABUNDANT LIFE IS YOUR BIRTHRIGHT.

All who are led by the Spirit of God are children of God. So anyone who takes their faith walk seriously should not behave like a cowering, fearful slave. Instead, we should behave "like God's very own children, adopted into his family – calling him 'Father, dear Father.' For his Holy Spirit speaks to us deep in our hearts and tells us that we are God's children (Rom 8:14-16 NLT).

The only way we can approach life in the manner described above is to believe that abundance is our birthright. Claiming our birthright means that we get to the point where we can state that as Christ followers, if Jesus came so we could have abundance, then we shall have it – period! This mindset is reflected in Paul singing while he was imprisoned, rejoicing while he was burdened by shackles. It is reflected in his writing the "joy letter" of the New Testament in the midst of the horrible circumstances and hopeless conditions in which he found himself.

The enemies of abundance are everywhere. In every circumstance, around every corner, we can find legitimate reasons why we should not feel that our cup runs over with the joy that Jesus desires for our life. Sin, depression, rejection – these are just a few of the things that can come between us and God, us and abundance.

But just as joy is not based on circumstances, abundance is not predicated on living a life free of difficulty. Difficulties, trials, and tribulation are part of the journey of life and there is no escaping that fact. But one of the primary steps in living a life of abundance is determining that abundance is our birthright and that we are meant to live a life of abundance. Abundance, then, is not a destination or something that we hope for, it is a part of who we are and something that we require each and every day. It is a "we will accept nothing less" perspective.

Every day we must move closer to our God. Every day we must move closer to our family. Every day we must move closer to our dream. Every day we must dream. Every day we must do Kingdom work because that is what God put us here to do. Every day, it is this type of life that we must wake up looking for. The abundant life becomes our expectation and the norm because it is our right, our birthright, as fully devoted, fully surrendered Christ followers.

Living the abundant life requires that our life be transformed from the inside out by the working of the Holy Spirit. It requires that we accept the grace, the love and the redemption offered to us at so great a cost. But it also requires that we make the determination to live the abundant life. There are steps we must take and things we must know, but our abundance pilgrimage will be for naught until we decide that we will live the abundant life and that we will settle for nothing less.

There are many hurdles to overcome if we are to live the abundant life. Many of these factors were discussed in detail in the previous chapter. But even amidst these trials we still have the ability to focus on the abundant life that we were put here to live and to move toward that life every day – no matter what. All of the obstacles can be overcome and we can live the abundant life that Jesus came to provide.

There is no easy road to abundance or toward anything that is meaningful. Championship teams must practice and spend quality time in the weight room long before they play in the big game. Orchestras have to turn the chaos of many different instruments into a collective harmony through hours and hours of individual and group practice. And marriage – wow – doesn't it require so much work to keep the communication, the intimacy and everything else moving in the right direction?

If the three major components of life – Faith, Family, and Vocation – require so much work, why do we expect that life itself would be any different? Life requires a great deal of hard work and the route to an abundant life takes considerable effort as well. We will not stumble or ease our way into abundance. We have to work hard at it and be prepared for the difficulties and challenges that we will face. When faced with those challenges we have to be prepared to overcome them. We cannot shrink from the task. Everyone wants to be an overcomer though until they actually have something to overcome. The reaction to the challenges of life will often determine if our journey toward abundance will continue or be halted by circumstance.

Quite frankly, abundance lies before us and is ours for the asking. Asking instead of taking because abundance is a gift provided by the life and sacrifice of Jesus. Asking instead of taking because we are not able to successfully chart a course to abundance on our own. Asking instead of taking because we need help from God in revealing to us what it is that He placed on our hearts to care about and to do with our lives. Asking instead of taking because without this knowledge being revealed to us by God, we will never truly find ourselves or our way in this world. We were made by and for Him. We will never be ourselves until we find Him and the reason He put us here.

But abundance is also for the taking. Because after we have these things revealed to us, after we come to know what it is that God put us here to do, after our eyes have been opened to the course that we are take, after all of this we still have to choose what we will do with the glimpse of abundance that is before us. Will we approach the ocean of abundance with a thimble or a tanker truck?

Asking for guidance from God on what abundance should look like in our own lives is the equivalent of looking upon an ocean of abundance. Receiving the information and then acting upon it by committing yourself wholly to the pursuit of God inspired abundance represents driving the tanker truck up and claiming as much abundance as possible. Which will you choose?

Jesus said that He came so that we would live abundant lives. He also posed a haunting question: "Why do you call me, 'Lord, Lord,' and do not do what I say?" (Lk 6:46 NIV).

Are you doing what He said? Are you living the abundant life? As you consider these questions let us continue to explore the characteristics of the abundant life. In the pages that follow I will draw a few pictures of abundance for you. The remainder of the book will then be dedicated to finding your specific version of the abundant life.

PERSONAL REFLECTIONS

Do you approach life as a conqueror, a child of the King, or as a victim? Elaborate.

Has the world ever convinced you to forget you are made in the image of God, that you are His favorite creation, and that abundance is your birthright? When? How?

Jesus said, "I have come that they may have life, and that they may have it more abundantly." Tommy Newberry said we "can walk up to the ocean of abundance with either a thimble or a tanker truck." How can you remind yourself to ask more of life, and to strive for abundance because it is your birthright? Who can you get to help remind you of this? How might that work?

ABUNDANCE IS DOING WHAT GOD WIRED YOU TO DO.

For we are God's workmanship, created in Christ Jesus to do good works, which God prepared in advance for us to do. (Eph 2:10 NIV)
   For this reason I remind you to fan into flame the gift of God … (2 Tim 1:6 NIV)

Have you ever seen someone who is either terrified or very uncomfortable speaking in public? Churches and corporations offer ample opportunity for the president of a board or department head to make presentations to an audience because of their title or role. Isn't it incredibly uncomfortable to sit through a presentation when someone is really struggling? Have you ever seen presenters stammer their words, lose their place in their notes, mis-speak several times, or sweat profusely? Deep inside we cheer them on and hope they get through it because it pains us to see them struggle so badly.

On the other hand, have you ever sat through a presentation with a gifted communicator who didn't really feel passionate about the topic that he or she was presenting? Although this person is a good communicator, you could detect that his or her interest level in the material was not high. The presentation comes across as impressive and polished, but not sincere. People might actually leave talking about how great a job the presenter did, even though he or she didn't really care for the heart of the material itself.

In one case, someone is doing something that he or she is not naturally gifted or inclined to do. In another, someone is using his or her gift – communications – but the message carried by that gift does not resonate within her soul. In either case, there is a separation between natural gifting, the work that is being done, and the impact of that work *on the one doing the work.*

Abundant living means that we finally give in and do what God has wired us to do. There are multiple discoveries that must be made as we determine what it is that we are wired to do. It is not an easy thing to figure out. Fortunately, it is possible to know that you are doing what you are supposed to do with your life based on how God wired you.

When you start giving in and focusing more and more on this "divine wiring" you will begin to tap into a level of life satisfaction that you may have never known before. Can you imagine the power of knowing – today – that you are acting on God's orders? That's getting your marching orders straight from the top!

It is very important to make a distinction here. Doing what you are wired to do does not necessarily mean doing what you are good at. The example above involved a gifted communicator delivering a presentation. Was she doing what she was gifted to do? Absolutely! She probably delivered a remarkable speech that her audience really enjoyed. Perhaps they marveled at her skill level. But was she doing what she was "wired" to do? I really don't think so. She used her gift, but not in a manner that fed her desire to do something significant, to really make a lasting impact. She was gifted to communicate, but our wiring goes deeper than just our gifts.

Our gifts are merely the medium through which our message is carried. Radio waves carry messages of many kinds, but I can't think of one person these days that will sit around marveling at the radio wave itself. What makes the radio wave meaningful is the message – music or words that are carried across it.

So it is with gifts, with abundant living, and with us. We have to ensure that there is consistency and a connection between all of these elements within ourselves so our abundance can grow. If we have the right gift but the wrong message or wrong work, there will be no abundance.

The businessman who is fulfilled when he is leading, encouraging, and building people will never be satisfied with the financial manager position that affords him title and higher pay but robs him of the chances to use his gifts. He will walk around with a smile but deep inside will feel the sad hunger that comes from knowing that he appears to be successful to everyone else, but does not feel that way about himself. Likewise, if you are working outside the realm of your giftedness you may get the job done, but will feel a similar disconnect when who you are and what you do grows farther and farther apart.

Being good at something has very little to do with abundance, giftedness or being special in any way. In fact, there are few things that any of us could not accomplish if we were consistent, persistent, focused, and committed to achieving our goals. We just start stepping toward the goal every day and refuse to stop until we are there.

But living the abundant life is different. Living the abundant life, where we literally overflow with the goodness and richness that God intended for us to have, requires that we approach life in a different manner. To live abundantly means that we must start by taking a look at our wiring. We must consider carefully how God put us together and what gifts, talents, and skills He used to complete the package. Then we orient our lives around that information.

> 1 Cor 12:12-27 (NLT) *"Now all of you together are Christ's body, and each one of you is a separate and necessary part of it."*

When we start doing what God has wired us to do, we will approach our days in a different manner. The excitement of going through a day knowing that you are doing what God wired you to do is absolutely incredible. The confidence that comes from that knowledge is unbelievably powerful. The feeling of making a significant impact, of having a personal and lasting influence on the world around us every day will cause you to get more and more committed to living life based on the wiring that God has provided.

Perhaps the single most important factor of abundance as it relates to God's wiring is this: You have to believe that you have been uniquely wired and uniquely gifted by the God who makes no mistakes. You have to believe that you are no coincidence and that you did not arrive where you are by chance.

This is a critical element of the abundant life. I see so many people who *believe in* God, but do not necessarily *believe* Him. They believe in God spiritually – Heaven, salvation, redemption, creation. They know that we are all sinners and fall short of the glory of God. They know that there is something within us that strives to do wrong even as we want to do right. They know that apart from the sacrifice of Jesus we could not appear pure and blameless before the Lord. These things they know – and they believe.

They also know that God gives us each unique gifts because we are told so in Romans 12:4-8 (NLT): "Just as our bodies have many parts and each part has a special function, so it is with Christ's body. We are all parts of his one body, and each of us has different work to do." They know that we are "God's workmanship, created in Christ Jesus to do good works, which God prepared in advance for us to do" (Eph 2:10 NIV). They know that Jesus came so that we "may have life, and…have it more abundantly" (Jn 10:10). These things they know – the positive aspects of our Christian walk – but for some reason they do not believe what God says we can do *with* that knowledge.

Why do I say they don't believe? Because true belief implies not only a cognitive recognition of the validity of what you are presented, it also implies that if you deem the information to be valid – true – that it will actually impact the way you think and act.

> *Rom 12:4-5 (NLT): "Just as our bodies have many parts and each part has a special function, so it is with Christ's body. We are all parts of his one body, and each of us has different work to do."*

We are presented with the negative aspects of ourselves and the means of redemption through Jesus. We hear these things and we believe. We are truly humbled, repentant, and thankful. We are presented by the Lord with assurances that we are divinely charged with impacting our world and gifted by the hand of God to do so. Do we respond by doing our part to change the world? Generally no. We simply choose not to believe that it may be us that is being tapped on the shoulder by the finger of God to go out and do great things – Kingdom things.

Why is it that we embrace the negative elements of who and what we are, but virtually refuse to truly embrace those potentially earth shattering, incredibly positive qualities that God has given us? I don't know where this disparate treatment comes from, but I hope to communicate a clear message to you: God has wired you to do incredible things and you are uniquely gifted to accomplish His purposes. He wants you to have meaning. He wants you to have joy. He wants you to approach each day with the same breathless excitement that comes when you lean over a ledge to admire the beauty and magnificence of a mountain range. He wants you to look at your wiring – the wiring He provided – and be excited and confident about the amazing things that He is going to do through you.

> Eph 2:10 (NIV) "We are God's workmanship, created in Christ Jesus to do good works, which God prepared in advance for us to do."

So, an indicator of the abundant life in action is that a person begins working toward and focusing on, what God has wired him or her to do. This step of doing what you are wired to do, whether you are a seasoned believer or just starting to figure it out, is one of the most critical, and perhaps most liberating, of all the steps in the journey toward the abundant life.

Living the Abundant Life

PERSONAL REFLECTIONS

■

What are you good at?

To what extent does doing what you are good at provide fulfillment?

What is something that you do well (or have done well) that glorifies God in some manner?

What has God wired you to do?

Describe the feelings you get when you are able to spend time doing what God wired you to do.

Do you believe you have been uniquely gifted (wired) by the God who makes no mistakes?

Do you believe that you are no accident and that you did not arrive where you are by chance?

Do you believe that your life and your contributions are supposed to be integral parts of God's plan?

You *believe in* Him – do you *believe* Him?

ABUNDANCE IS ABOUT LIVING TODAY — RIGHT NOW — TO ITS FULLEST AND IN THE DIRECTION OF YOUR GOD-ORDAINED PURPOSE IN LIFE.

If you have seen the *Rocky* movie series, you will surely remember when Clubber Lang (Mr. T) came to town as the ultimate bad boy of boxing. Rocky had gotten soft as the heavyweight champion and took Clubber far too lightly. As a result their first fight was brutal and ended with Rocky getting knocked out.

A scene that followed is so memorable. In it Rocky goes back into training camp with Apollo Creed as his trainer. Apollo tries to change Rocky's fighting style to get him into shape, mentally and physically, to get his title back. They are on the

Living the Abundant Life

beach doing sprint drills and Apollo, much faster than Rocky, leaves Rocky way behind. Apollo crosses the finish line and looks back to see that Rocky has stopped running.

Apollo approaches Rocky and pushes him to work harder. What is Rocky's response? "Tomorrow, tomorrow." Apollo goes nuts at that answer and shouts at Rocky. Apollo's response echoes in Rocky's ears as he looks at himself in the mirror in the next scene: "There is no tomorrow Rock, there is no tomorrow."

In many ways abundant living is taking to heart Apollo's reminder to Rocky. Abundant living means that we are no longer satisfied with waiting until tomorrow to start doing what God created us to do. We are no longer willing to wait until tomorrow to be who God created us to be. Abundant living means that we are not willing to put it off anymore. We start working toward it immediately. Abundant living might be well represented in the following quote by Barbara Sher in her book, *I Could Do Anything If I Only Knew What It Was*:

> *Now is the operative word. Everything you put in your way is just another method of putting off the hour when you could actually be doing your dream. You don't need endless time and perfect conditions. Do it now. Do it today. Do it for twenty minutes and watch your heart start beating.* [1]

It is a paradoxical existence when you start living the abundant life. Everything has to be right now, but your right now takes on a Kingdom perspective. You might have infinite patience about many things in life, perhaps even things that would have bothered you before, but now they just don't have the same impact.

On the other hand you will not be denied your daily dose of significance. You refuse to let a day go by without doing something related to your purpose for being. You absolutely refuse to wait any longer on the abundant life or living your dream.

Convinced that abundance is your birthright you determine

to take your place at the head table – immediately. I remember a mentor of mine telling me that you earn your spot at the table but you *take* your seat. Likewise, we must grow convinced that Jesus has earned the right for us to be at the table of abundance and that He actually wants us there. Because of that conviction we must not hesitate to claim our seat.

At the same time you must be willing to accept virtually any movement toward abundance. You must view progress toward the dream as proof of a day well invested, a day well lived. In other words, you become convinced that the seat at the table is yours, but you don't fall into depression and give up hope if you are not able to sit there today. If you come one step closer and make one realization that will help you get there, or grow in an area crucial to the accomplishment of your mission, you can regard it as a day of abundance. The angels are singing, the stars are in perfect alignment, and all is well.

Instead of focusing on the distance left to travel, realize that you are closer today than yesterday. This realization convinces your psyche of the undeniability of your mission. An important point to make is that "the table" at which you are striving to sit must be representative of your God ordained mission or purpose in life. If you set your sights on wealth, status, or self-aggrandizement, the day will come when that house of cards will crumble.

Linking our target to God's purpose for our life ensures us that we will always have a mission that will involve challenge, growth, risk and trials, but most of all significance. This is important, because more than anything, we all want to feel like our life matters, like we make a difference during our limited days on the earth.

So we live today to its absolute fullest and refuse to wait until tomorrow to start making progress. As we do that we keep God's purpose for our life at the forefront. This purpose is our driving force and the reason for our impatience. We essentially say, "God put me here for this, for today, not for the pot of gold at the end of the rainbow. I will live in and live out His will for my life today, right now. For this I came."

We can't wait for tomorrow – we won't wait for tomorrow –

because waiting makes us delay the gratification that comes from knowing that we are walking in the will of God. And though we may have struggled with the instant gratification of an impatient generation before, we now know that our impatience in this matter is of divine origin.

Abundance does not wait until tomorrow. Abundance does not wait for perfect conditions. Abundance does not need an invitation. Abundant living is aggressive living. Abundant living is jealous living. It absolutely refuses to accept any other manner of living and especially regards mediocrity as the enemy of that which is great and divinely inspired within us. Abundance is about living today, right now, to its fullest and in the direction of your God ordained purpose in life.

PERSONAL REFLECTIONS

Have you been guilty of waiting until tomorrow to truly start living?

What are some of the things you are waiting or have waited for?

What should you stop doing or focusing on so much so you can live the abundant life that God desires for you right now?

What should you be impatient for? What should you refuse to wait to do?

Jesus said, "A rich man had a fertile farm that produced fine crops. In fact, his barns were full to overflowing. So he said, 'I know! I'll tear down my barns and build bigger ones. Then I'll have room enough to store everything. And I'll sit back and say to myself, *My friend, you have enough stored away for years to come. Now take it easy! Eat, drink, and be merry!*' But God said to him, 'You fool! You will die this very night. Then who will get it all?' Yes, a person is a fool to store up earthly wealth but not have a rich relationship with God." (Lk 12:16-21 NLT) What does this say to you about waiting until tomorrow to start living the abundant life?

"There is no tomorrow." What Kingdom work are you doing today? What should you be doing now?

ABUNDANCE IS ACCOMPANIED BY HIGH ENERGY LEVELS.

Abundant living means doing what you are wired to do and doing it right now. It also means doing so within the framework of the purpose for which you have been put on the face of the earth. Both of these components essentially deal with the process of determining what abundance might look like in your life and then carrying out that vision.

Assessing your current level of abundance can serve several purposes. First, it can remind you of what you can look forward to when you gain clarification about the path your life might take. Second, it can help you affirm that the path you are on is leading to the abundant life that Jesus spoke of. Finally, it can be a wake-up call if you have been living a life of plenty but not one of abundance. In essence, the descriptions that follow can serve as goals to strive for or as simple yardsticks to measure your progress toward abundance.

A natural outgrowth or reflection of abundance in your life and mine is energy. If you are doing what you are wired to do and moving toward your purpose for being, there will be a clearly identifiable extra bounce in your step. Your eyes will not be able to hide their sparkle, the sparkle that emanates from deep inside of you.

Abundant living and energy will always have a high degree of correlation. If you are living an abundant life you will have an energy output equal to the task of abundance. It is not easy to do Kingdom work each day. It is not easy to take the task of every day living so seriously. It is not easy to stop being casual about the way you spend your days. To invest, not spend, as much of your time as possible is something that is extremely rewarding, but also especially consuming. It can wear you out. But when you are living this abundant life there will be something within you that will fuel the fire again and again, rejuvenating you and enabling you to strive for more.

The reason for this unlimited wellspring of energy in the abundant life is, quite simply, the source. Jesus offered the woman at the well, and us, "living water." When comparing the water at the well and the living water He said: "People soon become thirsty again after drinking this water. But the water I give them takes away thirst altogether. It becomes a perpetual spring within them, giving them eternal life" (Jn 4:13 NLT).

Picture the dried, cracked ground of an empty lake bed. It is perfectly suited for holding water but there is none of the life giving substance to be found. In desert regions it can be a sad symbol of loss as animals, clinging to hope in the dry season, go there only to die before the rains come. A few months later it will appear as though the region were the most bountiful on the planet. Yet another seasonal drought will come and the animals will perish in the same spot that earlier provided them with energy, sustenance, and life.

Ours is a similar scene. Those things in our life that seemingly provide meaning, but are apart from God, represent the seasonal pools of water. We focus so much on them and they provide us with meaning, entertainment, intrigue, and energy – for a time. But the seasons change, and all of the sudden, our oasis starts to shrink and a cracked, dusty bottom takes its place. Dust and water mingle to form an unsatisfactory mix in place of the cool refreshment we used to take for granted.

Times change. We grow up. The excitement of sneaking off and doing this or drinking that is replaced by a professional quest. Our pool fills back up as we drink from the well that our profession provides. So we work hard, start climbing the ladder of success, and for a time we bask in the glory of our rapid ascension. Then one day we're amazed when we see the pool has shrunk. The water that nourishes us is not as easy to get to as it was yesterday. The sale, project, or mission don't satisfy as completely as before. We're left to wonder what is missing as we see the dried ground overtaking more and more of our lake.

Throughout life we keep trying to fill this lake with sources that will eventually run dry. Over and over again the lake fills up and then starts shrinking. At some point we should step back and ask ourselves if we are the ones to fill the lake. Are we really up to the task? Are we qualified?

Jesus said what He gives will become "a perpetual spring within them, giving them eternal life." This perpetual spring is why energy must be reflected in abundant living. If I am living an abundant life, I have a perpetual spring of life within me. Picture that for a moment, particularly against the backdrop of the dried lake bed that our life so frequently becomes. The stream He provides never stops. It always flows and provides life-giving, life-rejuvenating sustenance. The amazing thing about this perpetual spring is that the source of the stream is within us. It gives life and eliminates the need for dependence on outside sources for abundance.

When you have this source flowing within you, if you have tapped into the wellspring of abundance, an outflow of energy will naturally become part of your countenance. Just as dams use the power of water to create electrical energy, so the streams of living water flowing within us produce energy that naturally emanates from us. So abundance will always be correlated to, or accompanied by, a high level of energy within the one living the abundant life.

As we consider the energy levels that accompany abundance, I think it necessary to consider the opposite. What if you don't have those energy levels? What does that mean? Go back to the three components of life – Faith, Family, and Vocation – and consider the holistic approach that we have taken to abundance. Specifically, the abundance that I am speaking of is reflective of a life nourished by the streams of living water that flow through every area of our life.

High energy levels in your Vocation do not necessarily reflect abundant living. Do you have the same energy level, focus, passion, and commitment in the realms of Faith and Family? High energy levels in your Faith walk are great, but do you bring any of that energy to your business pursuits or your Family? We are told to do our work as if we were working for God, not for man (Col 3:23). Do you bring this level of energy to your Vocation? The point is that your energy must be consistent and high throughout the different areas of your life. You cannot be imbalanced and call it abundance.

The abundant life is one marked by an overflowing of joy and the conviction that you are doing what you are divinely wired to do. The natural result of such a condition is that you will be continually refreshed by a virtually endless supply of energy. It will be evident in everything from your talk to your walk to the gleam in your eye, as the source of your abundance moves from external sources to the streams of living water that emanate from within you.

PERSONAL REFLECTIONS

How are your energy levels?

How has being a Christ follower increased your
energy levels?

Do you have a perpetual spring of energy that cannot
help but overflow into the world? How is it expressed
through your disposition and activities?

How has your relationship with Jesus changed your
energy, your joy, your engagement in the act of
living?

Do you have that perpetual spring within you? How
has this influx of energy changed you?

ABUNDANCE CHANGES YOUR DEFINITION OF SUCCESS.

In the previous section we discussed the positive correlation between abundance and energy levels. As abundance increases it will be accompanied by a corresponding rise in energy levels. Conversely, if you do not feel particularly energetic, you can rest assured that you are blocking your avenues to abundance.

Abundant living also brings more success than you might ever have imagined. But when you start living the abundant life your definition of success will change. Consider your definition of success to help differentiate "real" success from the way you might have once viewed it. This is so important, because over and over again, I observe the definition of success changing as people go through different life stages.

At 16 years of age success means getting a date, getting a car, and getting a driver's license. Graduating from high school and getting into college become other milestones, along with finding a husband or wife and starting a family. Completing college with the degree of your choice and getting started on your career become markers for success as you march down the road toward a professional life. As you get older, a comfortable retirement is another rite of passage. As the years go by, the measures of success continue to change based on what we have accomplished and what we have yet to do.

Although this sounds like a natural evolution as we go through life, there is an undercurrent that sweeps people away from the ocean of abundance as they go through this process. We are taught, or somehow discern, that success is measured by doing certain things, completing them, and then passing through to the next stage. We graduate from high school, then college, then get married, then get a job, then a house, car, big-screen TV, and so on. We experience one material success after another.

Please don't misunderstand me. I am not saying that abundant living means moving away from goals or significant events in life – quite the contrary. In fact, abundant living requires a focus on goal orientation, and it demands that those goals become the basis of everything that you do.

The difference between abundant living and material success is the unchanging nature of the goals related to abundant living. When you approach important goals from the basis of your natural wiring (what God put you here to do) there will be a consistency about your actions and your orientation that will carry you for the rest of your life. No longer will you depend on others' definitions of success. Instead, your relationship with God enables you to define your success in terms of the fulfillment you receive from living out your purpose in your Faith, Family, and Vocation.

However, success cannot be defined by a single element in any of the realms of Faith, Family, or Vocation. Success, as it pertains to abundance, must cross the borders freely between those elements so that success in one area is an affirmation of the total journey that you are taking.

What you are doing at work, and your impact there, will affirm your faith and must be consistent with your family walk as well. Your faith walk is thereby energized. It is alive, vibrant and lends itself to your family and vocational goals and pursuits in some manner. Your emphasis on family is reinforced – it is rooted in your faith – and is likewise carried over into your vocation.

That is real success. It is success that keeps your soul intact because it simultaneously feeds all of the components of life – Faith, Family, and Vocation. It is success that ensures a question that Jesus posed will not apply to your life: "And how do you benefit if you gain the whole world but lose your own soul in the process" (Mt 16:26 NLT)?

You may not control many of the outcomes of your efforts in life, but you have complete control over your journey toward abundance. Since the vast majority of your time will be spent on the journey, not at the summit, the quality of your footsteps should be your primary focus.

When you change your definition of success to ensure there is a Kingdom component that feeds and fulfills the different parts of your life, you will find a quality in your steps heretofore unknown. When you do this you will start accumulating daily doses of success and significance that will energize your every step.

PERSONAL REFLECTIONS

∎

What does success mean to you?

How have your definitions for success changed over the years?

How does it feel to have success in one area (Faith, Family, Vocation) and not in another?

Consider Faith, Family, and Vocation and explain how you would define success for each?

Success in Faith equals:

Success in Family equals:

Success in Vocation equals:

Can you be truly successful in life if you are not successful (by your definition) in Faith, Family, and Vocation?

What will determine if your life is a success in human terms?

How do you suspect that God will determine if your life is a success?

What might be a definition of success for your life that would stand the test of time?

ABUNDANCE WINS THE ROUTINE
BATTLE WITH FEAR.

And we know that in all things God works for the good of those who love him, who have been called according to his purpose. (Rom 8:28 NIV)

Do not be anxious about anything, but in everything by prayer and petition, with thanksgiving, present

Living the Abundant Life

your requests to God. And the peace of God, which
transcends all understanding, will guard your hearts
and minds in Christ Jesus. (Phil 4:6-7 NIV)

In the previous chapter we looked at the impact of fear in our lives. We fear rejection, we fear that people won't like us, we fear that people won't approve of us, we fear that we will look stupid, we fear that people will think we are nuts. The truth is we are confronted with situations that evoke a fear response on a daily basis. Fear is a natural thing – and a good thing – when it comes to warning us of dangers that lie ahead. But it is also one of the primary elements that keeps us from living the abundant life.

When you live the abundant life that Jesus came so you might have, the element of fear does not disappear. In fact, you could argue that fear might increase. As you begin your journey, there will be ample opportunities to stumble before you steady yourself. Also, as you strive greatly, full of confidence in your God-ordained mission, you will occasionally fail to reach the great heights that you were aiming for. These situations can cause fear to grow in our life. Fear is simply a part of our every day existence and there is nothing we can do to change that.

But when you start living the abundant life it signifies a change in the way you approach fear and adjust to its impact on your life and decisions. Since fear will be with you no matter what, you must confront it daily and ensure that it does not become a negative influence in your decision making process.

I well remember one of the most significant moments in my Naval career. As an Officer I was asked to submit a "dream sheet" that identified what I wanted my next job to be. As I studied the form I realized that during my enlisted career I had shied away from positions related to a certain aspect of shipboard life. The more I studied my behavior the clearer it became to me that fear was at the basis of my decisions – fear of people finding out that I didn't know something I should have known; fear of not knowing everything; fear of knowing too little about too much. So, on my "dream sheet" I indicated my desire for the job that would make me responsible for the very role that had previously caused me so much fear. This job would consist of my being responsible for the entire 327-person crew in this somewhat intimidating area. There would be no hiding from fear if selected for the position – and I was. I officially went from the frying pan into the fire!

What that assignment caused me to do was to deal with the fear that already lived inside of me. I had to decide if I was going to let fear run my life and make my decisions for me. A short time later I encountered a similar situation and it was much easier to make the decision to confront the fear rather than shy away from it.

So many times we let fear immobilize us and keep us from living the life that we should. The sad thing is many times we may be so close to making our dreams come true when we give in to fear. Most things worth having come with effort, pain, and trials. You must be willing to keep pushing forward even when you have encountered skepticism and self-doubt. Abundant living requires that you deal with fear on a daily basis. Heed what fear is trying to tell you without letting it stop you from doing what must be done.

Soldiers at the front let fear tell them to hit the ground when a certain noise is heard. Their brains, like ours, are wired with a "fight or flight" mechanism for that very purpose. But they cannot let fear run rampant and keep them from pushing forward. The soldiers' beside them, the families waiting at home and the country they serve are counting on their decision to conquer fear and keep moving toward the goal.

Likewise, God is counting on our willingness and ability to conquer fear. He wants us to keep striving toward abundance, toward Him and His purposes, each day. As we strive toward Him and His purposes we are strengthened by His promise that all we do will have meaning that lasts beyond today. "And we know that in all things God works for the good of those who love him, who have been called according to his purpose" (Rom 8:28 NIV). This promise assures us that there is meaning in everything we do, and that God is strengthening us through every event or circumstance. "In all things God works for the good of those who love him ..." as long as our purposes are in line with His.

Wherever we are there fear will be. But we must develop and maintain the ability to appreciate the presence of fear while at the same time ignoring it. Abundance and fear should not duel for your attention or compete in your decision making process. You must decide now to sweep fear aside and opt for the abundant life.

It is this reaction to fear that will keep your abundance growing. Likewise, your confidence in your God-ordained purpose in life will increase every time you overcome the immobilizing effects of fear by stepping out in faith. Abundance and fear cannot co-exist as equals. Abundance must consistently quiet any fears you face so you can continue to thrive and grow.

PERSONAL REFLECTIONS

Fear has an enormous impact on our life and on our pursuit of abundance, though we usually don't admit that to anyone else! What fears have you overcome and how did you feel when you conquered your fear?

What fears are inhibiting you now from doing what you want to do, what you need to do, to live the abundant life?

How would it make you feel if you determined – today – to overcome those fears?

ABUNDANCE IS ABOUT VICTORY BUT COMES ONLY AFTER SURRENDER.

If any of you wants to be my follower, you must put aside your selfish ambition, shoulder your cross, and follow me. If you try to keep your life for yourself, you will lose it. But if you give up your life for me, you will find true life. (Mt 16:24-25 NLT)

Abundance is about winning. It is about victory. It is about becoming spiritually bullet proof and impervious to the daggers the world hurls at you. It is this kind of winning witness that makes Romans 8:37 so applicable to the abundant life. Romans 8:37 (NIV) says "in all these things we are more than conquerors through him who loved us."

"More than conquerors" – doesn't that sound incredible? Don't you want that description to apply to you? The problem is all too often we seek victory, we seek to live as conquerors, without meeting the necessary prerequisites. A military force preparing for battle must train long before it engages the enemy on the battlefield if it has any real hope for success. A sports team must go through a rigorous preparation period to achieve the desired level of success.

All worthwhile endeavors are preceded by periods of intense preparation. It is during these periods that the battle is often won or lost. The engagement itself is simply a reflection of the preparation. Likewise, trying to achieve victory and abundance without taking care of the necessary prerequisites is like trying to play a game or fight a battle without adequate preparation. You may go through the motions and even look like you are in the game but you have no real chance for success.

What is the necessary prerequisite for abundant life? Jesus told us in Matthew 16:24-25 (NLT). "If any of you wants to be my follower, you must put aside your selfish ambition, shoulder your cross, and follow me. If you try to keep your life for yourself, you will lose it. But if you give up your life for me, you will find true life."

You cannot live the abundant life without surrendering your life to God's will. You cannot achieve victory unless you give up claim to yourself. You cannot become "more than a conqueror" until you have conquered yourself and put your life in the hands of the Master. What does that look like? What does putting your life in the hands of the Master look like?

I was at a leadership conference listening to the late Bill Bright of Campus Crusade for Christ. He was in frail condition, wheelchair bound and on oxygen to sustain his life. He described the hospital visit in which he was diagnosed with a fatal condition.

A nurse explained his condition and he placidly accepted her information. Not convinced that he understood the gravity of the situation, she went into more detail. She gave specifics about the degenerative effects of the condition, the painful treatments, and finally the grim certainty of death. Still, there was little reaction from Bill. Finally, the nurse raised her voice and exclaimed, "Don't you understand me? Your next breath could be your last one!"

Unshaken, Bill Bright smiled at the nurse. Confident and composed, he said, "What an honor to know that I may be one breath away from the Master." Twenty-five hundred of us in the audience dropped our jaws in unison. We applauded this giant of a man as we heard his amazing testimony. He was the embodiment of surrender, faith, and courage.

This man was a lamp for Christ. He did everything he could to be more than a conqueror for his King. His accomplishments were amazing. Yet amidst the glory that could be gained from having such an impact on the world, he clearly lived with Jesus at the center of his life.

Did Bill Bright have a major impact on the world? Yes. Was he immensely capable? Yes. He had an amazing impact on countless millions of lives through Campus Crusade, the Jesus video and other endeavors. There is no question about it.

Yet he was quite content to describe himself as a slave of Christ. He was quite content to celebrate that he may be with the Master in the next moment. He even admitted that the thought was quite enticing to him. Bill Bright embodied what it means to surrender his life to the will of God.

Surrender is when your entire perspective changes. Every event, detail, and situation in your life is viewed and processed against the backdrop of God. Everything you do and everything you are is related to God.

Contrary to many opinions, surrender is not a passive process. I was speaking with a friend who shared how difficult it was for him to "let go and let God" take control. He said he knew he was supposed to let it all go but he struggled mightily in trying to do so. I do not believe that "letting it all go" is the goal or the nature of surrender. Surrender is not passive.

Surrender is Jesus praying with fervor that the cup of suffering would be taken from Him and then, moments later, praying that it would remain if that were the Father's will (Lk 22:42). Surrender is Jesus overturning the moneychanger's table because He was too consumed with righteous indignation and the will of the Father to sit still. His lashing out was a result of His surrender (Jn 2:13-16). Surrender is Peter preaching after he had been ordered not to because that was his calling (Acts 4:18-20).

Surrender is Jesus giving a command to Peter – a fisherman – about fishing that flew in the face of what every fisherman knew. Instead of ignoring the command or accusing Jesus of not knowing anything about fishing, Peter said, "Master, we've worked hard all night and haven't caught anything. But because you say so, I will let down the nets" (Lk5:1-5 NIV). "Because you say so, I will" is the statement of surrender that Peter gave to Jesus.

Surrendering a life to God does not mean giving up control. Actually, it's quite the contrary. Surrender means controlling every moment of every day and ensuring that the direction of everything that we do or say is toward God. Surrender means that "we take captive every thought to make it obedient to Christ" (2 Cor. 10:5 NIV). We don't let go. We take words, thoughts, and deeds captive and place them at the foot of the cross.

Why so much emphasis on surrender? Because abundance requires surrender and surrender is the first step toward abundance. While He walked with us, Jesus said again and again, in various ways, "Follow me." And that remains His message today. As we start looking into the components of the abundant life one theme will ring true over and over again. We have to keep our spiritual antenna tuned for that voice that is speaking directly to us. We have to listen for the voice of the Creator of the universe as He whispers our name and beckons us toward our calling.

It is useless, though, for us to listen for Him, pray to Him, or do anything else that might invoke His name if we are not willing to give up our claim to the title of God. We have to stop thinking and acting as if we can handle things just fine by ourselves. Surrender means nothing less than saying that God is God and that we are not. We must affirm to ourselves, "God is in control and I am not. God is the God of the universe, and I officially and permanently declare myself unsuited for the task. I am free to simply do whatever it is that He places in my heart to do at the very moment that He says to do it."

Surrender means that I don't have to force things anymore. It means that I don't have to manufacture my destiny, my purpose, or what kind of impact I am to have. Surrender means I acknowledge that God created me to have some kind of magnificent impact on this world and that I am giving Him permission to use me to do those amazing things with and for Him. Surrender means I am willing to do "whatever" God wants me to do "whenever" He wants me to do it – no matter what. Surrender means I believe God has created me on purpose and that I trust His purpose for my life. Moreover, it means I believe finding and living out His purpose for my life is my primary objective. It means I will let nothing come between that objective and me.

If the world throws up road blocks I will drive through or around them or wait until God clears the road block on His time. My job is to keep my eye on the destination and to keep moving in that direction – no matter what.

It means trusting God enough so that if I can't see the destination or where the road leads, I will continue the journey if my relationship with Him verifies He sent me in that direction. Whatever He wants me to do is what I will do. My job is to keep moving in the right direction and to stay surrendered to God. It means affirming, "Because You say so, I will" whenever I have important decisions to make and actions to take.

Surrender means that the destination is not mine. It means that the speed of the journey is not mine. It means that success or failure is not mine. Surrender means that you and I are simply doing what we are told to do by the Creator of the universe with the faith that His guidance is sufficient for us. God is God and I am not – and that's okay –"Because You say so, I will." Until we have this commitment to surrender, we cannot expect to have a more than conqueror type of victory. Abundance is about victory, but it is always preceded by surrender.

PERSONAL REFLECTIONS

Do you consider surrender to be passive (giving up) or active (giving in)?

Is your life surrendered to Jesus? Elaborate.

What shackles do you need to break free from in order to live a surrendered life?

Do you have a "Because You say so, I will" relationship with Jesus? If not, why not?

Would you be able to say, "What an honor to know that I may be one breath away from the master?"

WHAT IS THE ALTERNATIVE?

What is the alternative to our current lifestyle? The alternative is to realize that Jesus came so that we might have life and have it more abundantly. The alternative is the determination that you will live an abundant life – no matter what.

Once this occurs you can begin to experience mask-free living. Who you are can remain constant in your Faith, Family, and Vocation. You will stop thinking that abundance applies to someone else and instead accept it as your birthright as a believer. You will feel the confidence that comes from doing – and knowing that you are doing – exactly what God wired you to do and to be.

Walking in God's will for your life will no longer be something that you put off until tomorrow. It will instead be satisfaction that you receive from today. You will experience the high energy levels that come from tapping into streams of living water – from within! You will find your definition of success is modified and placed in a more eternal, unchanging, and spiritual context. You will routinely win in the battle with fear – even those fears that you alone know that you have.

Finally, you will understand the freedom that comes from truly giving up your claim to divinity! You give up trying to rule the world, even your own world, and let God be God. In doing so you take captive every thought, word, and deed and wrestle it to the cross where it is submitted to Jesus for His guidance and direction. You willingly surrender to the One who made you and loves you more than you can imagine. You are finally free to just do what He tells you to do and make the following incredible statement a true reflection of your life: "Because You say so, I will."

Sometimes it seems as though we forget the promises of our Lord. Sometimes it seems as though we forget that we are His most cherished creation. Sometimes it seems as though we forget that He promises life more abundantly and wants so badly for us to experience that life. But the stirrings in our soul and the promises of Jesus remind us that there is another way to live. Let us now continue the journey toward the abundant life that awaits us.

CHARACTERISTICS OF ABUNDANCE

- Abundance is mask-free living.
- Abundance is determining that the abundant life is your birthright.
- Abundance is doing what God has wired you to do.
- Abundance is about living today, right now, to its fullest and in the direction of your God ordained purpose in life.
- Abundance is accompanied by high energy levels.
- Abundance changes your definition of success.
- Abundance wins the routine battle with fear.
- Abundance is about victory, but comes only after surrender.

PERSONAL REFLECTIONS

How many of the "Characteristics of Abundance" are reflected in your life?

Which are not? For each, why not?

Do you live an abundant life right now? If not, what is holding you back?

How would it make you feel if the characteristics of abundance described in this chapter described your life?

Do you want to embody each of the "Characteristics of Abundance?" If Jesus were to show you the way would you say, "Because You say so, I will?" Would you willingly surrender?

3

PASSION

The glory of God is man fully alive. Saint Irenaeus

In the last chapter we defined some of the characteristics of the abundant life and identified "surrender" as the most important prerequisite for abundant living. We will now look at those elements that must be in place if we are to build the kind of life that embodies the promise Jesus made to us in John 10:10 "I have come that they may have life, and that they may have it more abundantly."

A life that embodies the abundant living message in John 10:10 will be different for each child of the King. This is because our relationship with Jesus is a personal one. Each of us is invited into a personal relationship with Him, and that relationship ushers in the surrender to His will for our life and into our specific calling.

The remaining portion of this book is dedicated to a discussion of those "Elements of Abundance" that form the building blocks of the abundant life. Discovering these elements is necessary, because too often, children of the King accept the sacrifice of Jesus and are redeemed but are unclear about how to convert that acceptance into the victorious, joy filled, abundant life that John 10:10 promises. Understanding the "Elements of Abundance" in your own life will help you make that transition and capitalize on the incredible promise of John 10:10.

To live an abundant life, you must first *live*. To truly live means far more than just going through the motions of daily living. To truly live, there must be engagement of the soul. Something deep inside of you must be touched and nurtured in order for that spark of life to be fanned into flames. The flames we are looking to create represent the first element of abundance – Passion.

If you are incredibly successful in your job and are not fulfilled, you do not have abundance. You can have the greatest family life in the world and yet have something missing. You can even love the Lord and contribute to your local church family, yet be plagued with a feeling of emptiness that you cannot fully explain or escape.

I was talking with a senior Human Resources manager recently who commented on how so many people go through a mid-life crisis in their mid 30's. Interestingly enough this may be the time when people have really started achieving significant successes, career and material.

The timing of those events is more than just irony. So many times we climb the ladder of success only to find that the view is not as great as we expected. We reach the pinnacle, but do not even have time to enjoy it before those old feelings of emptiness catch up with us. We are left to wonder what is missing but feel guilty about that train of thought. We have so much, why should we complain? Yet we cannot deny that something is just not right.

What is often missing is our passion for life. Many people have lost their sense of purpose. Living without purpose means they are breathing but don't really know why. This begs the question: Why are you breathing? Why do you bother? Aren't those incredibly pessimistic questions? But think about co-workers, friends, family and neighbors. Ask yourself these questions as you picture them in your mind: What are they living for? What lights their flame? Have they found their calling?

How many people do you know so well that you could answer these questions? How many people do you know who live such spirit-driven, ignited lives that their passion comes through in everything they say and do? How many people know what their calling is? Do you know?

Living the Abundant Life

I believe these are some of the most powerful questions we can ask ourselves: What am I passionate about? What do I care deeply about? What is it that lights me on fire and simply will not let me go?

Knowing what gives you energy means knowing what your passion is. Knowing what your passion is means you are getting closer to the reason that God put you on the face of the earth. We will cover passion in more detail in a moment, but I want to point out one of the primary reasons that it tops the list when we look at how to live an abundant life. Passion is the first element of abundance because it is one of the first signs that we are honoring our calling. It can also be one of the first things we lose.

When you listen to babies announcing their mealtime, or children playing, or observe young men and women maturing into adulthood, you will see clear signs of passion. But as we mature we accumulate layer upon layer of cultural expectations and etiquette. We learn how to be "proper" and composed instead of passionate. Passion is replaced by political correctness, conformity, and the strict adherence to the status quo.

I will be the first to admit that we all need the positive effects of socialization. We usually have to "tone it down" when it comes to the passion of our youth. The problem is we go too far. We bridle our passion and stifle our enthusiasm. To the outside world we may appear to have it all together, but no one is aware of the tumultuous waves rolling through our hearts and minds every day. There is an inferno raging within us. We don't know what to do with our inner hunger. We just keep pushing it further and further beneath the surface. Because we are convinced that a failure to control these emotions means we are social misfits we continue to act as if they are not there. We get better at concealing our feelings by pretending everything is just fine.

Meanwhile we die inside. We lose the zest in life. I believe that what we refer to as the mid-life crisis may be pent-up passion that escapes in childlike ways. It expresses itself as uncharacteristic immaturity, failure to take responsibility, jumping from job to job, moving from spouse to spouse, inability to work and play well with others, the list could go on and on.

There are two central themes that may be found at the core of many of these crises. The first theme is that there is an artificial quest. Someone has usually lived based on a construct of the world that may be fading rapidly. All of their life they may have been laboring under the illusion that they are in the center of it all, that the world somehow revolves around them. It is quite shocking for many of us when we realize that the world does not indeed revolve around us. It is alarming for some to know that the entire universe is not waiting to hear their opinion. It is especially difficult if we harbor these illusions as we enter our 30s. That is when this pent-up passion ushers in a mid-life crisis in the lives of so many people.

The second theme at the core of our crises is that our mid-life crisis may not be that much of a crisis after all. Our mid life crisis may simply be something within us asking a few of the questions we had "socialized" out of us so many years ago. The questions: What is my passion? What stirs me? What fuels my soul? What is it that the hand of God has placed on my heart and wants me to care so deeply about that I will commit a large portion of my life to pursuing?

Passion is vital because so frequently we cover all of the bases except our soul. We take care of our job, we take care of our wife or husband, we provide for our children, we even take care of our Bible reading plan. But we fail to take care of our heart. We fail to nurture our inner fire. We fail to develop the capacity to feel like we are doing something that is really making a difference in the world. All the while our soul is stirring, crying out for more, keeping us ever aware that something is missing and that it will not be satisfied with less than abundant living. It will not settle for less than our God-ordained calling.

That is where passion comes in. Passion makes our soul cry "yes." Passion makes us feel like we are pursuing what God put us on the face of the earth to do. Passion makes us feel like nothing else matters except pursuing our abundance. Passion makes us willing to take risks and gives us the courage to eliminate obstacles in our quest to be what He wants us to be. It makes us ambassadors for the abundant life.

Passion makes us pray: "Lord, let me try to do what You want me to do, accomplishing it or not is up to You." Passion makes us comfortable in saying that if we died tomorrow we would be fulfilled because we know what God has put in our hearts to care deeply about. We would find peace in knowing that we did everything we could to satisfy that passion. Living passion enables us to say: "I did my best," and be content with that statement.

But we cannot do what God has put on our hearts to do until we start listening to our hearts. We must honor the passion of our calling if we are to fulfill our calling. Without passion we will not be content with life, or ourselves, or become the person God wants us to be.

There are far too few people who know what it feels like to have their cup overflowing with abundance. Without God-ordained passion the world may think we are doing fine, but we cannot fool ourselves. If we are not attuned to our passion, we will find ourselves going through the motions and suffering from an incredible and growing emptiness.

Passion fills that void. Passion lights your inner fire and will not let you go. Passion epitomizes the statement, "For this I came" because it tells you clearly, succinctly, whether you are on the right track or not. Passion is one of the warmest blankets you will ever find. It can literally make you feel content even on the coldest of nights because you have the stirrings in your soul to keep you warm. Without passion your emptiness will cry from the mountaintops and the coldness that you feel will come from a passionless void deep within. True passion is not a fleeting sensory response to stimuli. It is a deep aching inside that bubbles up in the form of an energetic, enthusiastic, spirit-filled pursuit of life.

PASSION — THE MISSING INGREDIENT

How many people do you know who are passionate about what they do? They eat, sleep, and breathe – that special something! When you see them they will get the conversation to a certain subject. When you hit on that subject their eyes light up, flames shoot within them, they sparkle and dance. Every neurotransmitter in their body fires That is passion.

The great preacher John Wesley, when asked how he attracted such large, energetic crowds stated: "I set myself on fire and people come to watch me burn."[1] Like Wesley our impact on the world is at the apex when we are on fire about something. We spend so much time chasing quasi-passions – a sport, a companion, a title – we rarely stop to realize what a real calling feels like. We need to discover our passion – what God caused us to care so deeply about. That is the beginning of abundance.

Unfortunately, many people secretly give up on finding their passion and in so doing they give up on life. Personally, professionally, spiritually, they go into *pain minimization* rather than *abundance maximization.* Their goal is not the fulfillment of their soul, but to stop the pain.

If you look you will see the incredible impact and beauty of passion burning inside of someone who understands his or her Faith, Family, or Vocation walks. Mother Teresa worked in dirty, disease-ridden hospitals, ministering to the poor and changing the world. Michael Jordan won championship after championship by combining phenomenal talent, an incredible work ethic, and red-hot passion for his profession. Martin Luther King, Jr. turned a brief speech at the Lincoln Memorial into a Dream that can never die, because he was too consumed with the message to stay within his allotted time! Billy Graham continued to preach crusades year after year, when he could have been in North Carolina enjoying his beautiful mountain home. All of these people had "callings" which required that they spend their lives expressing who they are – passionately and faithfully.

Living the Abundant Life

PASSION —
THE GREAT MODERATOR

Passion, above all else, is consuming. There is no such thing as lukewarm passion. It either burns within you or it doesn't. With this in mind, I would like to share insight from my part time job at a psychiatric hospital while I was in college. I will never forget two of the most striking things about the clients I met there. First, they were not markedly different from the rest of the population. They could have been people I saw everyday in school, at work, and on the street. They were just average folks. Second, the biggest difference I noticed between them and the rest of the population was their response to the "speed bumps" or minor difficulties of life. For these wonderful people every minor issue was a major catastrophe. It kept them in a constant "tailspin" and robbed them of their quality of life.

I tell that story because passion is also "the great moderator." When you are so focused on something that it becomes the driving force in your life, your perspective changes about things that used to trouble you. That does not mean difficulties go away. But the impact of the trivial will be moderated, toned down, by passion's influence. When passion takes hold, your perspective is changed and the things that put you into a tailspin yesterday simply will not matter as much today.

The reality is that the world presents a model of living that suggests we should be loaded down with incredible baggage all of the time. It seems that if you walk around without an active neurosis you are not in vogue. My mother describes the time she told my brother, who was living out of the country, about some difficulties she was encountering at his farm. She was surprised at his nonchalance and pointed out that he did not seem very concerned about what was a pretty big issue. Steve's tongue-in-cheek reply provided keen insight into the human psyche. He said: "Mom, it's not that I don't care about that, I do. But, I just have enough problems to keep me happy right now." Wow! Steve was right. We tend to wallow in our problems and get everyone we know to wallow around in there with us. We can grow so content with our predicaments that they become a central and ill-advised security blanket of sorts.

In the corporate environment I have frequently said that if you want to solve people's problems you should start by helping them become more successful. Success, and the positive momentum it creates, tends to change people's perspective on problems. They forget all about them! All of a sudden the important *few* begin to take precedence over the trivial *many*. The "important" bucket isn't that full while many of the things in the "unimportant" bucket just keep disappearing. Passion does the same thing for us on an individual level. It separates the important issues from the unimportant and keeps us focused on what really matters. It keeps the main things in life the main things.

Passion is the great moderator. It helps us determine what we really care about. Once passion grabs you, you cannot look at yesterday's problems in the same light. In the midst of difficult circumstances and difficult people, passion provides an internal compass for navigating the treacherous waters of life. Perhaps this is one of the secrets behind Henry David Thoreau's reaction to being held in jail for non-payment of taxes. Thoreau, who influenced both Dr. King and Gandhi, said of this horrible set of circumstances, "I could not but smile to see how industriously they locked the door on my meditations, which followed them out again without let or hindrance, and *they* were really all that was dangerous." [2]

Thoreau didn't elaborate, but I feel safe in presuming that "they," his thoughts and meditations, the things that made him dangerous *and* historically significant, were indeed his passions. It was these passions that transformed the circumstances of his imprisonment into a body of thought that would influence the world and dramatically improve the lives of millions of people.

Just as it was true with Thoreau, King, and Graham, it is also true of us. Passion from the same source resides in us and is available to help us accomplish the great things that God instructs us as His co-workers to do. But we have to find this passion before we can start doing real Kingdom work, because God does not want our work alone, He wants us. We must be consumed by God, and the passion He placed within us, if we are to give Him our all. For this to happen we must reduce the peaks and valleys caused by the minutiae of life and keep our focus on God. We must harness the power of our passion.

PASSION CAN CHANGE YOUR LIFE BECAUSE IT JUST MAY BE YOUR LIFE

In the previous section we defined passion's role in properly moderating the peaks and valleys of life. Prior to the awakening of passion, we are at the whim of many different circumstances and elements. Once we become impassioned, the great moderator goes to work and minimizes the negative affects of circumstances on our lives. But there is an element to passion that may seem contradictory to the "great moderator" label. As passion starts to work in our life it may be accompanied by another set of peaks and valleys.

To illustrate, I remember hearing that Princess Diana was extremely unhappy during the last few years of her marriage to Prince Charles. It appears she was never entirely comfortable with her role. An amazing transformation occurred when she started working with victims of land mine explosions. This became a driving force in her life. She helped make significant changes in how the world dealt with the whole issue of land mines.

That is the positive part of the story, the part where discovering her passion changed her life and impact on the world. Paradoxically, it is also probably true that she had never before grieved like she did after she developed this passion. Seeing the maimed children, disfigured adults, all of the consequences of land mines, simultaneously stirred both her passion and her pain.

Passion carves out a place in us, and by necessity, makes us vulnerable. It causes us to care more deeply. It enables us to feel more engaged, inspired and significant. But it may also cause us to experience the pain and disappointment that comes from caring so much. I am not sure if it is accurate to say that we care more. It may be more accurate to say that we are more fully engaged in life.

There is something within each of us that longs to care deeply and to have a great impact on this world. When I pray for my children I pray that they will know the amazing things that God wants to do through them. I don't pray for mediocre achievements. I see my children accomplishing great things and making a huge difference in the world. I pray that their faith, family and vocation walks will be of such magnitude that it will be pleasing in the sight of God.

We all dream of such a life. Then we wake up and our dreams have faded. Were we to try and remember what it was that stirred us so much the day or night before we probably could not. The noise level is so high in our lives that the thoughts and dreams of greatness and those passions being stirred in our soul by the God who put us here cannot fight their way through.

Too many people allow their grand thoughts, thoughts of greatness, to be followed by mundane periods that numb them into forgetting those thoughts. They repeat this process day after day and eventually stop believing that they are capable of such great endeavors. They deny the possibility that such an existence, such a passion, such a life, could be theirs. John Eldredge comments on this by saying, "though we try to resolve the dilemma by disowning our desire, it doesn't work. It is the soul's equivalent of holding our breath."[3] We cannot keep holding our breath and expect life to be any different.

Do you ever have those days when you're a little down but you don't know why? Author, psychologist, and Nazi death camp survivor Victor Frankl indicated that his patients frequently complained of being tired all week long, but on Sunday they were faced with boredom and, sometimes, depression. He described this "Sunday neurosis"[4] as the result of feelings of emptiness or meaninglessness – signs of just "marking time" through life.

I do not know the validity of Frankl's observation, but I believe there is some truth to it. Sunday afternoons can have a bitter irony about them. I look forward to the weekend as a time to answer to no one (or almost no one!). A busy Saturday comes and goes, as does Sunday morning at church. All of the sudden Sunday evening is upon me and I am left wondering where it went. On those particularly slow Sundays, do you sit around and wonder if this is it? Preparing for the week ahead, do you ever wonder if this is what all of the work is about? Is this the reward? We feel trapped because we are not entirely happy at work and there is something missing at home.

Passion is the overflow of our hearts innermost desire. It is often what we are missing when we wonder about what is missing. It is the knowledge and use of our passion that allows us to feel that we are doing what we were put on earth to do. The size of the hole that is left unfilled within us is too great to ignore if passion does not exist in our life.

We are wired for passion and something within us dies when we do not nurture and exercise it. Life requires that we breathe; it doesn't require that we do much else. Passion can change our life because it may be our life. It may be the foundation of what we were placed on earth to do. Knowing and expressing our passion helps us ensure that we are giving life everything we have. It means we will never have to say on our deathbed, "I wish I had only ..."

PASSION CAN MAKE A WAY

What is in your heart? What makes all time stop and your attention become so focused that everything else is rendered meaningless? What is it that truly lights the fire within you? Many people do not know the answer to those questions and that is just sad. Sadder yet are those who know exactly what keeps the flame burning, but are unwilling to venture out and bring their dream to life.

I believe that passion perplexes, but it also provides. Passion can burden and confuse you. It can be frustrating to have a passion with no apparent means of satisfying that incredible hunger. But passion also provides the way to satisfy that hunger.

Jean de la Fontaine said, "Man is so made that whenever anything fires his soul impossibilities vanish." I believe the author is right. Do you challenge impossibilities or just sink into a routine – not pushing forward, not challenging, not pursuing? His declaration also begs the question: Has anything fired your soul?

The very thing that will make impossibilities vanish resides inside of you. God did not create you to "mark time" on earth. He did not create you in His image to just go through the motions. Jesus came so that we might have abundant life, but the first thing we have to do is engage in life enough to start the journey toward abundance. There has to be something that lights the fire within us – a righteous passion – if we are going to walk in concert with the God of the universe. There will be no abundance if we are not walking in this manner. But if we really have a passion, as opposed to a passing fancy, that passion will eventually find a way.

PASSION –
WHAT DO WE DO WITH IT?

So far we have talked about the importance of passion and what it can do for those who embrace it. Hopefully, if we stopped here, there would be a good understanding of the power that passion can have in our lives.

So many times when I talk with people about passion, and its vital role in life, I see the spark of realization shining clearly in their eyes. They readily acknowledge that something is missing, and the thought of something missing consumes more of their time than they like to admit. They admit they have lost their passion for life, that something has slipped away somewhere down the line. They know what getting it back could do for them.

But then they think of their current existence and fail to see what role passion plays. They like the idea of having a passion that consumes them, but do not know what their

Living the Abundant Life

passion could possibly have to do with their current job. They don't know how their spouse, friends, or employers would accept it. They see the need, but they hesitate to unbridle their passion.

Hear me clearly on this: *Understanding your passion and living with it as a major driver in your life has absolutely nothing to do with your current existence.* Imagine this: You finally understand what God has put in your heart to care deeply about. You come to grips with the fact that your being on the face of the earth has something to do with your passion. But you look at your job or life situation and fail to see how your passion has anything to do with your current situation. So you give up on what God put in your heart and keep going through the motions of life. In so doing you accept the huge hole in the middle of your soul as a permanent fixture. Is that a reasonable solution?

Of course not. To think that we would give up on God's design for our life instead of a worldly plan that moves us away from Him and toward mediocrity is a ridiculously ludicrous thought. To be clear, I do not believe God, work and abundance are mutually exclusive. God put Adam and Eve to work in the Garden of Eden, and I believe He wants us to work, too. But if we could only walk one path, I hope we would pick God's path and not the material path.

Not finding your passion in life is the same as not finding life itself. For those people who are caught up in the external trappings of success – artificial, temporary measures of gratification – that may seem fine. But there will come a time when those who neglect their passion will lay on their deathbed and wonder what difference they could have made in this world or for God. I hope we all can answer, "I did my best" and have that statement apply to the most meaningful areas of our life.

After coming to an understanding of the role passion plays in life and abundance, you must commit to finding and living out your passion. One of the things you must realize, as you begin the search for your passion, is that it must be related to the whole of life, not just individual areas. Earlier we broke life down into three components and labeled those paths Faith, Family, and Vocation. When you start looking for your passion, you must focus on integrating all three of those important areas into your Kingdom work.

There are many components of work that frequently trap type "A" personalities like me into thinking we are tapped into our passion. I have worked with plenty of people who were incredibly driven about achieving success and moving an organization up the earnings or stack-ranking chart. There is nothing wrong with that. I have been with those people and have been one of those people. But earnings potential, the bottom line and worldly success may have little to do with glorifying God.

I know parents who have settled into a life that entails going through the motions at work so they can give all of their time to their children. Their stated passion is their family and they give everything they have to that family. The thought is noble and in many ways I stand in admiration of those who think that way. But the reality is many of these people suffer from a pretty severe "empty nest syndrome" when the children move out of the home.

Their children are not their reason for being and neither is their family. Their reason for being is to glorify the God who put them here. Their "job" is to act upon the world He created in concert with His designs. Any parent's responsibility is to show their children what a man or woman of God looks like who is on fire with the passion He put in their hearts.

Our faith walk can and should be the most empowering source of confidence and energy in the entire world. I once heard a Navy Admiral say that he never met a true Christian who made a bad Officer. I am inclined to agree wholeheartedly. We should have power and confidence in our vocation because of our faith. In reality though, we can justify our way into thinking that it is enough for us to love God and help our church. We can convince ourselves that our job does not mean so much because it is not related to our image of Kingdom work or what we deem to be the really important things in life.

Please forgive me for a moment as I remind you that

Living the Abundant Life

everything in life is Kingdom work if we are working properly. We are to do our work as if we're working for God, not man, and it does not matter if we are doing what we want to do or love to do. We must be the best street sweeper, ditch digger, CEO or technician we can be because in everything we do, we are representing the Master.

The point of these examples is to emphasize that our passion must cross the boundaries of Faith, Family, and Vocation. Whatever is in our heart to do – whatever God put there – we must find a way to apply it in all of the different areas of life, because our passion represents who we are at the core of our being. Otherwise we backslide into our masks and take a U-turn from our abundance. The road to abundance begins with finding the God-inspired passion that makes the crooked roads straight and the straight roads filled with abundance.

FINDING YOUR PASSION – HOW DO YOU START?

I heard someone say we are all products of one or two major themes and we just keep going back to those themes over and over again. Passion would have to be one of those themes for me. Since I am always ready to talk about the need for passion, I have become pretty accustomed to what people have to say about the topic.

Most people understand the need and desire for passion in our life with relative ease. I have never encountered anyone who wanted to argue about the value of having a life passion – something that serves as an eternal flame within us.

Most people agree they need it but have no idea how to find it. I was talking with a friend about passion one day. For a number of years he had struggled with finding out what he was supposed to do with his life. As we spoke I explained my belief in the power and necessity of a passion. He admitted that he was essentially bored with life and wondered if this was all there was to living. During the conversation he became more interested in the necessity of passion. Then he asked the haunting question that is the most common response I get from a serious discussion about passion: "How do you find your passion? I don't even know how to start."

We don't find our passion because we are not encouraged to look at our career and our life from the standpoint of what God put in our heart to care deeply about. We don't discover our passion because we are too busy chasing the golden ring: a new job, the next promotion, or financial security. Passion eludes us because we spend our life so wound up we think rest is the reward.

We don't find our passion because somehow, someway, along the journey we have been distracted so successfully that we forget we were made for the passion. Our passion represents who we are and what God put in our heart. Finding our passion, and living it out, does not represent the highest level of achievement in life. Rather, it represents the basic building block of a successful life – an abundant life.

You were wired for passion. If you do not find out what your particular passion is you will never truly be "home" in your life. You will always live with the knowledge that something is wrong – that life is somehow not how it should be – that there is something missing even though everyone else thinks you are doing just great. You can usually fool other people, but you cannot fool yourself.

The first thing you have to do when you start looking for your passion is know what you are looking for. So often when people start looking for their passion they think they must find something that changes the world. They look at world hunger, they look at the multitudes of unsaved souls, they look at curing cancer, and they look at pressing global issues. The problem with this approach is as soon as you record it on paper you may realize that your chances of impacting those things on a large scale are very, very small.

Because the task seems so large you may conclude that the pursuit of large goals – Kingdom goals – is best suited for other people. What a tragic conclusion! Kingdom work is for everyone. You may very well be a person who changes the world, so I can't say what you are passionate about won't make a huge difference. But before you change the world you must first discover your God-inspired passion without thought of what you will do with it. God's designs, combined with your obedience to His call, will determine how your passion is employed. Your responsibility is to discover the passion He placed in your heart so you may be attuned to that call.

For example William Wallace, the character Mel Gibson plays in the movie *Braveheart,* has to be considered one of the most passionate, driven characters to grace history. After his wife was brutally murdered, he was forced into a conflict with the English and finally played a major role in liberating Scotland from English rule though he would not live to see the day of liberation.

Throughout the movie Wallace finds himself on the battlefield trying to convince his fellow Scots to fight for their freedom. But what was he really fighting for? The easy answer is to say that he was fighting for Scottish freedom from English rule, that his passion was a free Scotland.

I believe the answer runs deeper than that. What drove Wallace into conflict was his unwillingness to submit to unjust rule. He was willing to fight and die for that principle. He fought the British for the freedom of individual towns and villages long before it extended into a wider conflict. The principle of freedom took him from town to town before it drove him to deal with two countries. Eventually, he was caught by the British, and although he was tortured, he would not succumb to crying out for mercy. He chose freedom instead of compromise from those who tortured him, even as he died.

So what was William Wallace's passion? Was is a free Scotland? No, I do not think it was. A free Scotland was what William Wallace wanted to do *with* his passion; it was the application of it. His passion was freedom! Long before the concept of a free Scotland entered his mind the passion surging through his veins was freedom – period. As his life took the turns that all lives take many things changed about how that passion was applied but the passion on his heart never changed. His final word, cried out with his last breath, was indeed the passion that epitomized his life – "Freedom!"

Another champion of freedom was Dr. Martin Luther King, Jr. He had advanced degrees, the Nobel peace prize, and many awards of distinction from his years of courageous service. But what was his passion? He told us clearly what it was when he preached the sermon that became his eulogy. He said that he wanted us to think of him as a *drum major:* "Say that I was a drum major for justice. Say I was a drum major for peace. Say I was a drum major for righteousness. And all of the other shallow things will not matter."5 In many cities across the country, and during the conflict in Vietnam, he found himself involved in struggles that tapped into the common themes of justice, peace, and righteousness. Even some of his early childhood memories – like the one of his father being publicly humiliated by a white police officer – can be directly related to his passion for racial equality.

Martin Luther King, Jr. was a man of passion who did so much good for so many people. But I believe his passion started with those basic elements of justice, peace, and righteousness that were burned indelibly on his heart as a child. His passion was justice, his passion was peace, his passion was righteousness. What he eventually did with those passions impacted many different cultures, people, and countries.

The first thing you need to know when you start looking for your passion is that you are not looking for what you do with your passion – we will get to that later. You have to discover what is in your heart. You need to put aside plans, other purposes and anything else until you come to grips with what God has placed in your heart to care so deeply about.

A QUEST FOR PASSION

As I began my quest for the abundant life, I realized the topic of passion was the first thing I had to tackle. Like many people, I struggled to find my passion because I was looking for something bigger to do, some big problem to solve, instead of focusing on what God put in my heart.

So I examined my Faith, Family, and Vocation to determine

what brought out my passion in each area. What was it in my work that made me feel like I was doing something that fueled my soul? What was it in my relationship with my wife and children that made me feel like I was giving them the best I had to offer? What was it that made me feel I was really doing Kingdom work and building my relationship with Jesus?

I asked these questions and compared the answers from one walk of life to the other. I looked for common themes underlying the experiences that elicited a passionate response from my heart. As I studied the commonalities, I began to discover and understand my passion.

I found that no matter what I was doing, no matter where I was, I would be completely energized if I could talk about, read about, study, discuss or teach on the subject of leadership. The topic of leadership fuels my soul and literally has not allowed me to go to sleep at times. I can never get enough of it. So leadership was pretty easy to pin down as my first passion.

Identifying leadership as a passion was a meaningful discovery, but I knew there was something else. I looked at those times in my Faith, Family, and Vocation when I was most fulfilled and realized the relevant, passion-evoking experiences had another common theme. I realized that I am addicted to connecting with and uplifting people. I love engaging in deep, meaningful conversations with people. Anywhere, anytime, I love connecting with people.

Not only do I enjoy connecting with people, I want to lift their spirits. I want to help them feel a little better when they leave than when they came. I try my best to help them see a little more hope for tomorrow than they saw when we began our conversation. Consequently I'm a person who is constantly trying to encourage people to wish upon a star and to never give up. So my second passion was connecting with and lifting people.

In my Faith, Family, and Vocation I am at my best when it involves something related to these passions, because that is what God put in my heart to care so deeply about. I believe this is part of God's fingerprints on my soul. I can only feel at home in life and in my pursuits when I give in to those righteous impulses by tirelessly pursuing the passion He placed on my heart.

So as you search for your passion I encourage you to look for what it is that makes your heart beat faster. What is it that makes you feel fulfilled? Look at the times you felt fulfilled – in your career, in your church, in your family, even in something as small as a single activity or conversation – times when you were really touched deeply and led to care so much that your heart was fully engaged. Write those times down and study them. Look for the common themes that are present. It is these themes that will form the cornerstone of the abundant life that Jesus came to provide and that we must pursue as Christ followers.

PERSONAL REFLECTIONS

For the following questions make sure you apply the "needle in the haystack" method. It's easy to say "I don't find any satisfaction in my ___." (You fill in the blank.) But that's usually not the case. Many times we struggle with some areas of our Faith, Family, and Vocation, but we can pick out seemingly small things in each that really provide us satisfaction and fulfillment. Those small things may be the "needle in the haystack" that represents the common theme that speaks to your heart – your passion. Don't neglect the smallest details! Ask yourself:

In my Faith walk, what have I done before or what could I do that would bring me fulfillment?

What is it that brings me a deep sense of fulfillment and engagement with my family?

What about my Vocation fuels my soul? What are those moments, even isolated moments, when I feel that I am fulfilled or deeply satisfied in my vocation?

What is it I think about that makes me come alive?

What is it that I am doing when everything seems right in the world?

If I could teach all of the young people in the world one thing, what would it be?

Someone once asked the famous Methodist, John Wesley, how he attracted such large, energetic crowds. He responded: "I set myself on fire and people come to watch me burn." What lights you on fire? What creates so much heat you can't hide it?

What is your passion?

PASSION AND THE NECESSITY
OF A BURDEN

Passion is the first element of abundance. We have talked about the need for it, elevated it to an esteemed position, and explored how we can find it. It is indeed a powerful element in the search for abundance. But it is time that we put passion in its proper place.

For all of the power and influence passion has it is probably the most destructive element when it comes to living the abundant life. You cannot live the abundant life without passion, without something that fuels your soul, but you also cannot live it with unbridled passion. When passion goes unchecked, your distance from God and from the abundant life that Jesus came to provide increases exponentially.

I have detailed some of the historical figures that have accomplished great things, Kingdom things, because they spent their life giving in to their passion. It is also true that misplaced passion starts so many people down tragic pathways each year. Fathers are left without their children, mothers lose their husbands and their way, children have only one parent to kiss goodnight – all because of misplaced passion.

The alcoholic longs for his liquid passion, but the cocktail creates distance from his family and from God. Later that night he will probably say and do things that would be unimaginable during sobriety. And it all started with a misplaced passion.

I believe so strongly that God put within each of us a craving to care deeply and to make a lasting impact on this world. God wired us so that the first object of this passion, the first object of this desire, would be – God! That is why He told us "you will seek me and find me when you seek me with all of your heart" (Jer 29:13 NIV). God wants us to live from the heart in pursuit of Him. When we do that He will point us in the direction He would have us travel. We are hard wired for that passion.

Make no mistake about it, passion will express itself in our life in some form or fashion. Either we will have the passion that comes from God or we will eventually succumb to an unsavory substitute. Misplaced passion will turn us off so completely from the world and from God that we will be of no use to either.

The trouble comes when our quest for passion is filled by something or someone other than God. When we seek to fulfill our passion by anything other than God and what He puts on our heart, we are doomed to failure and destined for collisions in our personal life that will resemble the carnage left at the scene of train wrecks.

Have you ever talked with someone who has recently been face-to-face with a "train wreck" in his or her Faith, Family, or Vocation? I think the most appropriate description of the common reaction is this: "How did I get here?" The husband who loses his family over an affair can't believe how he got there. He can't believe it came to this. The businessman or woman who engages in shady practices can't believe it when the curtain falls, as it always does.

The couple that files bankruptcy. The pastor who disappoints a congregation with his sin. The "train wrecks" go on and on. They are caused by the ease with which we displace God-inspired passion with fleeting, worldly substitutes.

The problem is these "fleeting substitutes" leave God completely out of the picture. Adolph Hitler had a passion for Germany and Germans, but the absence of an anchor – a spiritual burden – led to unbridled and ghastly uses of that passion.

WorldCom and Enron executives probably had a passion for building their empires. Devoid of a moral compass, though, and lacking proper checks and balances, their misplaced passions led to their downfall and tragically affected the lives of thousands of innocent investors and employees.

The lesson is this. All passion, all true passion, all God-inspired passion, is rooted in a spiritual burden. And that burden is directly related to God and His purpose for your life. In Matthew 16:24 (NLT) Jesus told His disciples, "If any of you wants to be my follower, you must put aside your selfish ambition, shoulder your cross, and follow me." The burden in which our passion is rooted represents the shouldering of our cross as we follow Jesus.

Our burdens are necessary because passion, though a requirement of abundance, is far too dangerous when left to its own devices. We cannot trust the heat of passion or our own whims. We must tie that passion to a burden that points directly to the King and will always remind us of how we are supposed to use our passion.

Because of this I consciously ask myself some questions related to my passion on a regular basis: I can lead, God wired me to lead, but am I leading in a Godly manner? Am I leading for His glory or mine? I can connect with people. I can lift them up and encourage them, because God wired me to do those things. But when I connect, what is the goal? When I encourage, what am I trying to accomplish?

I lead, I connect, I lift, but am I glorifying God with the passions He placed on my heart? I know that passion without a burden as its root can too easily go astray, and be satisfied by a multitude of suitors. To build the abundant life I must cultivate God-directed passions.

Our passions must have a Godly burden as the anchor to keep them from drifting. If your passions are not God-directed, I would encourage you to think, pray and determine if they really are healthy passions. If it does not point to God in some manner, is it really worthy of committing a large portion of your life to pursuing?

FINDING MY BURDEN

When I determined what the anchor point was for my passion (leadership: connecting with and lifting people) and how it related to God, I discovered what truly made my heart leap for joy or cry out in anguish. My burden is "the lack of victory, joy and significance in the life of God's children."

My passion is leadership and connecting with and lifting people; and I am convinced that God put that motivation on my heart. My burden keeps me anchored to God and helps focus my passion in a direction that is consistent with His plan for my life. Thus, I don't want to "just lead" or "just connect" or "just lift." In my Faith, Family, and Vocation I want to lead, connect, and lift so that children of the King live more victorious, joy-filled lives. I want to lead, connect and lift in a manner that helps do something with the glorious burden that God has placed on my heart.

I cannot stand it when I see children of the King living depressed, defeated lives. I cannot bear to watch when I see someone who is a Christ follower showing all of the signs of one who has lost the battle. I love to lead. I love to connect with people. I love to lift people. But everything I do in applying these passions must relate back to my God-ordained burden.

I am convinced that if someone needs leading, needs to understand how to lead, or needs to be lifted, then they must go beyond me to the One who came so they can have an abundant life. There is a wonderful life of abundance waiting for someone – perhaps only a conversation away – and I have been privileged to have been part of some of those conversations. The Holy Spirit may have connected us for that very purpose so I am always preparing myself for these "chance" moments.

That is the proper use of my passion. It is my passion but it is not about me. My burden, my cross, is from God, directed toward others, and is an absolutely wonderful burden to have. And that is what we all must have in our life and in our own specific relationship with Jesus. If we seek Him and His guidance with all our heart He will take our passion and apply a burden that keeps us on the path He wants us to follow. That path, as we will continue to explore, has many different turns. But when we travel using His directions, His guidance, His passion and His burden, we will start to have His abundance in our life.

PERSONAL REFLECTIONS

What is your God-inspired passion?

When we seek to fulfill our passion by anything other than God and what He puts on our hearts, we are doomed to failure and we are destined for "train wrecks." Have you seen or heard of someone with a passion similar to yours who went through a "train wreck?" What happened?

What are the dangers associated with your passion? How could it be misused?

All true passion, all God-inspired passion, is rooted in a burden and that burden is directly related to God and His purpose for your life. In Matthew 16:24 (NLT) Jesus told His disciples "If any of you wants to be my follower, you must put aside your selfish ambition, shoulder your cross, and follow me." The foundation of our burden is the shouldering of our cross as we follow our Lord. What makes your heart leap for joy or cry out in anguish?

How is that joy or anguish related to God? How
is it related to the Kingdom?

Our passion determines what energizes us and
pushes us forward. Our burden reminds us that the
direction that we must always travel is toward God –
everything must glorify Him.

What is the cross that you have been called on by
God to shoulder?

What is the relationship between your cross and
your passion?

What is your burden?

Passion is more than a passing fancy. It is more than a
fleeting emotion that changes as we mature. Passion is who
we are. Passion is what is on our heart to care so deeply
about. A life surrendered to God's will results in the overflow
of divinely inspired passion in the heart of a child of the King.
Passion is God's fingerprint on our soul. Passion is the first
element of abundance. We cannot live the abundant life that
Jesus came that we might have unless we are actively
engaged in life. We cannot confuse the act of breathing with

the art of living the abundant life.

Passion stirs us so deeply because we are wired to be passionate beings. To drink deeply and often from the well of life instead of dabbling in the stagnant pools alongside the road is our calling. In order to drink deeply, we must engage more than our thinking self, we must engage our heart and soul in the act of living out our everyday existence. We must find our passion because we cannot truly live unless we live from the heart. C.S. Lewis pondered, "How can we hunger and thirst for righteousness when we have stopped hungering and thirsting all together?" We must maintain our ability to hunger and thirst. We must find and feed our passion.

Once we find that passion we will feel more empowered, like life really matters. We will believe we are doing what we are wired to do. When that happens we must take the time to ask what burden God has placed on our heart, what cross He wants us to bear, because that burden must serve as the anchor to our passion. Passion with burden as its root always points to and glorifies God, the Author of both our passion and our burden. As we find and use our passion rooted in our burden, we will be on the road to achieving two of life's major goals: Living the abundant life that Jesus promised and moving closer to God who so longs for us to live in relationship with Him.

What has God placed on your heart that fuels your
soul?
What is it that ties your inspired actions
to the Kingdom?
What is your passion?
What is your burden?

4

VISION

"If you had permission to do what you really want to do, what would you do? Don't ask how, that will cut your desire off at the knees. How is never the right question; how is a faithless question. It means "unless I can see my way clearly I won't believe it, won't venture forth." How is God's department. He is asking you what. What is written in your heart? What makes you come alive? If you could do what you've always wanted to do, what would it be?"[1]

Passion as we discussed in the previous chapter, is the first element of abundance. Before we try to do anything of significance in life, we must determine what it is that fuels our soul. Once we gain awareness of this critical element, we are left with another question: What will you do with your passion? To answer that question, we must turn to the second element of abundance – Vision.

Why is Vision necessary for abundance? Because living the abundant life means we are living intentionally. We are living life on purpose and striving toward what we are wired to do. Having a vision for life is necessary because without a vision we may travel in any direction and believe we are going somewhere just because we are moving.

Movement is not enough. Movement does not denote movement toward God or our true self – what we are wired by God to do and to be. Having a vision for our life guarantees we are moving in the direction that He would have us travel.

God made us to be His fellow workers and to do things on the way to our divine appointment with Him. As we fulfill our purpose for being here, we become truly ourselves. In order for us to be ourselves we must actively and intentionally live with a God-ordained vision as a central theme. The power and clarity of such a life is the result of a vision refined through prayer, study, contemplation, trials, failures, experiments, wrong turns, and recalibration. It does not just happen.

AN EXERCISE IN VISION

Imagine for a moment that you and I are on the same work team. We are trying to close a deal that everyone has worked on for months. We have received a phone call from our client saying that she would like to meet with us tomorrow morning to finalize the deal.

Our office is located in Jacksonville, Florida and our client is located in Fort Myers, Florida. There are no flights running to Fort Myers this evening, but we have a rental car. We need to get on the road immediately, so we can get there and start preparing for our meeting.

For illustrative purposes, let us consider the relationship between passion and vision. In this case, our passion for the sale may be the reason we are going on the journey, the impetus to action. The reality, though, is that passion is not enough. Knowing what we are supposed to do, what we are wired to do, and even what we are called by God to do is not enough. There must be a journey, a moving toward that destination. And before there can be a journey, there must be a vision about where we are going in the first place.

In our example, let me outline some of the steps we might take to get from Jacksonville to Fort Myers:

(1) *Determine where Jacksonville, Florida is on a map.*
(2) *Determine where Fort Myers, Florida is on a map.*
(3) *Identify the route to take from Jacksonville to Fort Myers.*

(4) Determine exactly where I need to go in Fort Myers.

(5) Estimate the time for each leg of the trip and the total driving time.

(6) Start driving.

Before we start a journey, we need to ensure that we know where we are. I cannot plan a trip to Fort Myers unless I know exactly where I am right now. If I don't know that, I can't get started. The second thing we must know before we begin the journey is our destination. I know you would figure these things out before you started your trip. You would not drive out of town in the nearest direction available thinking that you would figure out where Fort Myers is once you were on the road. You would also determine how long the journey would take before you left town. Those are the basics of going somewhere – anywhere, right? My question is this: Where are you going today, tomorrow, next week? Why are you "driving" down a particular road? Did you head out of town without knowing where you were going?

As you've probably guessed, I'm not talking about our exercise anymore. I'm talking about your life. Take a moment to answer the following questions:

Throughout this chapter we will examine the visions you have for your life, but we must first assess where you are right now. Max DePree said, "The first responsibility of a leader is to define reality."[2] In leading ourselves, we must look at the reality of our current situation and use it as the first critical reference point from which we travel.

Passion deals with the most basic issues: Why you breathe; what you were wired to do; what is it that lights your inner fire? The correct interplay between passion and vision can only begin once you gain greater clarity about your passion.

Once you have that clarity, your journey toward abundance can gain the crucial momentum it takes for long-term success. I heard once that "Passion fuels vision and vision focuses passion." I like to think of vision as working *out* what passion has worked *in*. Passion grabs us and lights us on fire. But we can just sit there and burn, burn, burn until vision comes along. Vision clarifies our passion. Vision shows us what we can do with our passion and the difference we can make. It shows us what is possible, that we are the ones who can make it happen. Andy Stanley describes vision as a "clear mental picture of what could be, fueled by the conviction that it should be."[3] I would propose that it is impossible to get really focused on a vision unless there is some passion involved to provide the "conviction that it should be."

WHAT IS VISION?

In many ways the term vision has been mystified to such a degree that it has lost much of its impact. Someone who is "way out in left field" might be called a visionary along with anyone else who seems to be a little bizarre. Modern business leaders are heralded as being visionaries, but are usually afforded that title after their journey is complete or at the twilight of their careers.

The problem with that is there are so many of us who believe in the benefits of a vision, but we are uncomfortable associating with people who are called visionaries. We are wary of the bizarre ones, and the ultra-successful leaders seem to be so far beyond our level that they somehow do not seem real. Let's be honest. Do you really see yourself in a dialogue with Jack Welch about business philosophy and strategies? We see the visionaries, but they seem so unlike us that we disassociate from both the individual and the idea of being a visionary.

So we continue to live in our own little world, apparently satisfied with living for today and without a compelling vision for tomorrow. We just go through the motions. Conversely, we might spend so much time fighting life, fighting to change everything or fighting to keep things the same, that we never think about next week. We can get so frantic in our attempts to alter today that we have nothing worth giving to tomorrow. We can help counter both of these false realities with a God-ordained vision.

What is vision? Vision is more than just a preferred tomorrow. **Vision is a clear picture of a distant future built** upon the foundation of intentionality and solidified by the successive realization of movements toward that future.

Vision is a clear picture of a distant future...

Having a vision means that the status quo is not good enough. To have a vision means you have decided there should be changes in the way things are. Martin Luther King, Jr. had a passion about inequality that began forming early in his childhood. His vision, what he would do with that passion, formed over time. I believe it came out in some respects during his famous "I Have A Dream" speech:

> *One day the state of Alabama, whose governor's lips are presently dripping with the words of interposition and nullification, will be transformed into a situation where little black boys and black girls will be able to join hands with little white boys and white girls and walk together as sisters and brothers. I have a dream today. I have a dream that one day every valley shall be exalted, every hill and mountain shall be made low, the rough places will be made plain, and the crooked places will be made straight, and the glory of the Lord shall be revealed ... with this faith we will be able to hew out of the mountain of despair a stone of hope.*

This vision, the beauty and symphony of the speech, had its birth early in Dr. King's life, but developed over time. Likewise, when vision is firmly established in your mind the picture becomes clearer over time. It is a picture of the future, a picture that has more clarity with each day it is pursued. But the only way to gain that clarity is to constantly look at the picture. What appears fuzzy initially will begin to take shape as you focus on it, study it. Eventually it starts to evolve into a coherent picture. Unfortunately many people give up and never focus long enough to reach that point of clarity.

I am reminded of some guidance I received about making

successful sales calls. I was told that most sales occur after the fifth call on a business prospect. The problem was most bankers never make the fifth call. Instead they tend to give up when they fail to close the sale on the first, second, or third call. They give up on the process too early and lose the opportunity to win significant business.

In sales, you become quite familiar with rejection. Yet you do not give up because you understand that a "no" today can evolve into a "maybe" next month and a "yes" six months later. But such success requires frequent touch points and a willingness to keep looking for glimmers of hope amidst the ever present chorus of rejection. You simply have to keep digging in. You have to keep going back to the prospect who told you "no." You have to persevere, believing that sooner or later you will make the sale.

Oftentimes the sale can seem anti-climactic. We celebrate for a brief moment, but then move to the next quest. We rejoice for a time, but often fail to study the process we used to achieve success, a process that required that we work through uncertainty and a lack of clarity before we achieved the goal.

Repetition, focus, redundancy, and perseverance are as critical for us today as they were for the visionaries we hold in such high esteem. If only we would take some of the lessons learned from our everyday experiences and understand that we must approach our God-ordained Vision with the same tenacity and dogged pursuit. We have to keep praying for the vision with confidence that God honors our intentions and hears our prayers and requests.

Jesus illustrated through a story that when we pray repeatedly for what we are seeking, our prayers will have impact. They will not fall on deaf ears. Luke 18:1-7 (NLT) records:

One day Jesus told his disciples a story to illustrate their need for constant prayer and to show them that they must never give up, "There was a judge in a certain city," He said, "who was a godless man with great contempt for everyone. A widow of that city came

*to him repeatedly, appealing for justice against
someone who had harmed her. The judge ignored her
for a while, but eventually she wore him out. 'I fear
neither God nor man,' he said to himself, 'but this
woman is driving me crazy. I'm going to see that she
gets justice, because she is wearing me out with her
constant requests!'" Then the Lord said, "Learn a lesson
from this evil judge. Even he rendered a just decision in
the end, so don't you think God will surely give justice
to his chosen people who please with him day and
night? Will he keep putting them off?"*

If we fail to see the vision at first, we must pray constantly
for guidance, for clarity, for insight, for wisdom, and never
cease striving toward the vision. God will honor our
persistence and intentions by bringing clarity to our vision.

Dr. King's vision, no doubt, had more clarity in 1963 than it
did in 1956. As he stayed the course and worked toward his
vision, the struggle brought the vision into clearer focus. I had
a similar experience in writing this book. A passion to convey
a message led me to start writing. However, I was not entirely
clear about what or why I was writing when I began. I
experienced frustration upon frustration and wondered why I
was spending so much time pursuing what often seemed
difficult to quantify. Frankly, sometimes I just wanted to quit.
But time and again the vision became clearer with each stroke
of the keyboard. Each time I begrudgingly worked through my
frustrations I moved one step closer to the vision that
consumed me. Vision gains clarity as we fight through the
"ambient noise" that seeks to distract us from our Kingdom
work and lead us back into mediocrity.

Vision deals with more than the near future. Vision is
much broader than merely tomorrow. It is a strategic direction
that has more to do with your legacy than the next 24 hours. A
vision that has tomorrow alone as its destination is not a God-
inspired vision. A true vision, a life vision, is about a distant
tomorrow and God-inspired work.

Nehemiah had a vision about rebuilding the gates of

Jerusalem. But the magnitude of the vision was much greater than just a construction project. Rebuilding the gates would help restore the symbol of strength and remind the people of their unique calling as God's children. But there seemed to be no way that the vision would materialize – it was just too tall an order.

Nehemiah was working as a cup bearer to the King when his vision came to him. His vision was for a distant future, a big event – a God event. His vision was so large that if God did not intervene it would not come about. Franklin Graham calls this "God room." God-ordained visions must be of the sort that we cannot bring them about through our own efforts – we must have God's help. We must give God room to work in and through our life. Nehemiah hung on to his vision. He gave God room to work and his vision eventually became a reality.

Your vision and mine will take different forms as we pursue it, but please don't limit your vision to the temporary frills of today. Make sure you are capturing the God-inspired vision that resides within all of us.

Vision is a clear picture of a distant future built upon the foundation of intentionality ...

Vision is built upon the foundation of intentionality. This means that vision is about intentionally moving in the direction of your preferred future. I remember being awe struck by the description of Jesus as He prepared for his return to Jerusalem, knowing that He would face His death on the Cross. Luke 9:51 (NLT) tells us that, "As the time drew near for His return to heaven, Jesus resolutely set out for Jerusalem." Resolutely set out for Jerusalem? Did He know what was waiting there? Of course He did. Ready to face the lashing, the humiliation, His death, He "resolutely" honored His calling.

Being intentional, going somewhere on purpose, is so critical when it comes to a life vision. Living life on purpose, living out what God has put us here to do, does not just happen. Except for rare occasions we do not stumble upon our central purpose in life. Rather, we come to understand it through trial and error, tears and laughter, good times and bad. All of our trials are put into proper perspective by God's incredible love for us. As we come to understand that love and our heart opens to His guidance, we start getting glimpses of what He wants to do with our life. We realize it is His plan, not ours!

We have to wrestle with the world and not let go of God. We must keep a steadfast focus to get to the point where we can say, "For this I came." Ironically, I have found that we have to maintain the focus on our purpose for living even after we have grown confident in such matters.

We must do this because we tend to fall by the wayside. As we discussed in Chapter 1, there are many variables that can distract us from the path of abundance. We get tired, we grow afraid, the "noise" keeps us from hearing the true sound of our King. Luke describes this malignant worldly process very well. He warns us:

> *When an evil spirit leaves a person, it goes into the desert, searching for rest. But when it finds none, it says, 'I will return to the person I came from.' So it returns and finds that its former home is all swept and clean. Then the spirit finds seven other spirits more evil than itself, and they all enter the person and live there. And so that person is worse off than before. (Lk 11:24-26 NLT)*

The translation is both simple and stark. There is nothing more threatening to the evil one than a Christ follower who is cleaning up his house and finding his way. The enemy will work overtime to keep you down, and his efforts are never more focused than when we start to believe the battle is won (1 Cor 15:54-58), we are a necessary part of the battle (1 Cor 12:12-27) and we are more than conquerors (Rom 8:37). Being intentional, going somewhere on purpose and refusing to stray from that journey, are critical elements of living out a vision.

Vision is a clear picture of a distant future built upon the foundation of intentionality and solidified by the successive realization of movements toward that future.

Vision is solidified by the successive realization of movements toward a certain future. Visions are rarely achieved in one fell swoop. We seldom know exactly where we are to go when we begin the journey. Instead, visions grow clearer through our intentional act of surrender to the Lord. They crystallize through the passions He places on our heart, through the burden that links those passions to His work, and through our constant quest to learn what we are to do with those passions.

True vision is the ability to see the future from the perspective of what could be and should be. With vision you are also able to see today in the proper context as it relates to the future. Any movement toward the distant future – the vision – is a successful journey. Each step, each "successive realization of movements toward that future" means that I am not only proceeding toward my life vision, I am living it out as well.

I believe many people give up on a God-ordained vision because it seems too far away. The future they are striving to create seems to be too different from the present to have any hope of success. Because of this, we need to keep our focus on the vision while at the same time receiving our reward, our reinforcement, from any movement toward the vision.

By doing this, we no longer have what John Maxwell refers to as "destination disease." People suffering from this disease constantly see a tomorrow that would cure all of their woes today. With this train of thought they often become so fixated on the goal that they never take the necessary steps to bring it to fruition. The disease is characterized by a growing depression, despondency, or embitterment because the would-be visionary is not where he or she wants to be.

To counter these symptoms, we must have a vision for the future, but accept movement toward the vision as the necessary inoculation against despondency in the present. Movement in the right direction is cause enough for celebration. It is sufficient justification that today is indeed an incredible day. It might even be sufficient justification to say that this life, if it ended today, was indeed an incredible life.

THE COMPONENTS OF VISION

The proposed definition of vision starts with what is perhaps the universally agreed upon element of vision – the future. Vision always deals with a distant tomorrow that dictates our movements today. A vision-inspired future is one that we strive for in the hope that tomorrow will reflect what we envision today.

One of the difficulties I have seen with establishing a powerful vision is that people sometimes do not know what to strive for. Most people buy into the argument that they should have a plan for their life. They believe in the proposition that they should have a preferred future. But they have problems when they start trying to convert that agreement into something concrete that could become one of the primary driving forces in their lives. They have difficulty converting vision from a theoretical concept into something that is really applicable to their lives.

Because it is the second element of abundance, it is critical that we narrow our focus and dissect vision. Vision deals with many different areas of our life and has multiple applications. A little later we will consider the role of vision in our Faith, Family, and Vocation as well as the need for an overriding vision for our life. One of the constants about vision is that every vision – every true vision – takes into account three components. These components are destination, ideal self and impact.

Destination

Every vision deals with these questions: Where are you going? What do you want to accomplish during the number of years allotted to you? What are your dreams, aspirations, and indications of a life well lived? Every vision deals with destination.

Every vision must include a destination component to be a true vision. If there is no destination, there is no vision. That destination could be physical: Nehemiah wanted to rebuild the gates of Jerusalem (though the vision was much larger than just the gates). It could also be faith-based: To own my own company and spread the Word of Jesus in my company and with all of those with whom we do business. Whatever form it takes there is always a destination component.

The good news about a vision, a true vision, a God-inspired vision, is that our goal has as much to do with the path toward the vision as it does with achieving the vision itself. Getting there is God's business. Getting there is something we might not have much control over. Getting there may require marshalling resources and changing people's minds and turning people's hearts. The direction is our responsibility, making it to the destination is not. It is in the realm of the Divine – leave it to Him!

What is required of us is that we proceed along the path identified as ours to travel. While the destination may not be controllable, the path always is. We can and must choose again and again, day after day, to walk along that path and to stay in concert with the journey God designed for us.

In so doing we satisfy the destination component of vision in that we are moving toward the God inspired vision for our life. "For this I came" is not a statement that we can make only when we arrive "there." It is a statement we can make as soon as we know where "there" is and can confidently say that we are on the path. Vision always deals with destination and the journey toward the destination.

Where do you want to go?

If your vision came true, what would it look like? Where would you be?

Can you envision a tomorrow where everything that is in your heart was fulfilled? What does that tomorrow look like? Where are you when you are there? What is your destination?

Ideal Self

Vision is about destination, but there is so much more. Many businessmen and women figure out where they want to go in their career and strategically plan to get there. That is a vision of sorts, but not the type that I am referring to in this book.

True vision, the vision that leads to abundance, deals with both the destination and the ideal self. Where do you want to go and who do you want to be when you get there? So many times people are caught in the trap of only looking at where they want to go. They see a future opportunity and imagine what that opportunity would look like.

This type of vision has contributed to the apparent success of many people and will continue to do so. Unfortunately, it has also contributed to the disillusionment of many. What so many people fail to take into account is this: What will it take for me to get there? What will I be when I arrive?

An entrepreneurial spirit led to the rapid rise of a man I heard so much about when I went to work in Jackson, Mississippi. Unfortunately people speak differently about this WorldCom executive than they used to. He made it to his destination, but was he who he wanted to be when he arrived?

I worked with a Naval Officer once who seemed to be a "friend of the people." He would do little things to let the sailors know he recognized and appreciated their efforts. He had a great sense of humor and was the kind of officer we would all follow. Years later, I was privy to information about his disastrous stint as a Commanding Officer. He was a walking time bomb that suddenly erupted one day. He was fired for slamming a sailor against a bulkhead. Being a Captain was his dream. Being a Captain was his destination. I wonder if he ever considered what he wanted to be when he made it there? Was that really how he envisioned himself?

Consider another example. Suppose I work for a company of questionable repute, but have a God-given gift for leadership. And suppose further that I have a strong desire to be the CEO of that company. I may be driven to get to that position and there is certainly nothing wrong with that desire. But what will it take for me to get there? Who will I be once I am sitting on the corporate throne? I know what I want to do, but who do I want to be when I am finally able to do it? Which is more important? Jesus posed this question in Matthew 16:26 (NLT): "And how do you benefit if you gain the whole world but lose your soul in the process?"

Vision deals with destination. It deals with what we are supposed to do, the Kingdom work that is before us. To know if we are doing that work and when it is accomplished, we need to have a clear picture of what our vision looks like when it comes to fruition. We are told in the Bible that we will spend our lives in a constant state of flux as God grows us into the role we are intended to fulfill and the Holy Spirit moves us into a closer relationship with Him. As Max Lucado said, "God loves you just the way you are, but he refuses to leave you that way."[4] We must be prepared to move toward our destination.

But vision also deals with our ideal self. It entails keeping our soul intact as we move toward that destination. We must ask ourselves questions like: Who do I want to be when I get to my next position? Who do I want to be ten years from now? Who do I want to be when I am old? What do I want my character legacy to be? What do I want people to say about me when I am gone? Vision is not only about where we are going, it is about who we want to be when we get there. It is about our ideal self.

PERSONAL REFLECTIONS

What character traits would you like to exemplify in your life?

How would you like those who know you to describe you?

What are you willing to die for? What do you live for?

Living the Abundant Life

> If your children were to write your epitaph or give your eulogy, what would you hope they would say?
>
> Where are you going and who do you want to be when you get there? What is your ideal self?

Impact

Where am I going? Who do I want to be when I get there? These are questions you must ask yourself. Every God-inspired vision must deal with these questions. Perhaps the biggest question that must be answered related to your vision is: What impact will you have on the world by carrying out the visions for your life?

Other important considerations are: In what ways do you want the world to be different because you were here? What will be the result of God having breathed life into your nostrils? Why do *you* matter?

I spent a number of years of my life on the bridge of a Navy warship. Earlier I mentioned a lesson I learned at sea called the "big ocean theory." This theory stated there was a strong likelihood you would not hit something in the middle of the ocean because it is, well, a big ocean. In the middle of that ocean I had many occasions to pause and reflect on just how incredibly large and powerful the seas were and how small and seemingly insignificant I was in comparison. But despite my smallness, despite my frailty, despite the seemingly limited impact I can have in this world, there are things I am supposed to do for and with God.

Ephesians 2:10 (NIV) tells me that I am "God's workmanship, created in Christ Jesus to do good works, which God prepared in advance for ..." me to do. By virtue of my relationship with God through Jesus, I am an important player in an unfolding Kingdom drama. And so are you! Our task is to change the world – at least a small portion of it. We are small, but we are also integral parts of what God is doing in the universe.

Before I was born, before you were born, there was something that God wanted us to do. Not collectively, not as a group, not as a people necessarily, but individually. We are all vital parts of His creation and are so loved by Him. There is no one who does not have a role to play in this Kingdom drama that is unfolding. Because of this I constantly ask myself two questions: What is my role? What impact does God want me to have on the world? One life at a time, one group at a time, one church at a time, one business at a time – all are good places to start. I know God is calling you just as He is calling me. He calls everyone to fulfill his or her God-ordained Vision in life.

Not everyone answers. Not everyone considers the vision of where they are supposed to go in their life – their destination. Too few consider who they want to be when they get there. Not everyone knows their ideal self. We often fail to distinguish between nice visions and God-inspired visions.

Your vision, and mine, if they are to be true ones, must lead to the abundant life that Jesus came to provide. Where we go, who we are when we get there, and the impact we have on the world defines our vision as either valid or invalid from an eternal standpoint. If we test our vision and find it lacking these components, we should not be surprised when our vision fails to fulfill our deep inner needs. When we identify our God-ordained vision, we will find that these elements are all accounted for, and all of the components are working together to propel us toward an abundant life that glorifies God.

Living the Abundant Life

In Ephesians 2:10 (NIV) we are told: "We are God's workmanship, created in Christ Jesus to do good works, which God planned in advance for us to do." Why do you suppose you were created?

What are the good works you are supposed to be doing?

What type of impact are you currently having on the world?

Is Kingdom work reflected in your current impact?

What impact are you supposed to have on this world?

A PERVASIVE VISION

Every vision deals with destination, ideal self, and impact. Your vision may be more heavily weighted toward destination while mine might focus more on impact. The weighting and specific balances will differ from individual to individual. But all visions must take these into account.

Just as important as the component parts is the need to have a God-inspired vision in the different areas of our lives. If you have a vision for your vocation, but none for your family or your faith, your vision will be skewed and unbalanced. It will be difficult for you to live the abundant life. As a matter of fact, there is simply no way you will. You must have a God-inspired vision for your Faith, Family, and Vocation if you are to live the abundant life.

VISION AND FAITH

When I do seminars, I frequently use the example I mentioned earlier in the chapter about driving from one destination to another. I ask the participants to determine how to get from one place to another. Then they present their directions to the rest of the participants. After we have heard the directions, we look at the decision making process they employed. It becomes clear that people start off with where they are, and then proceed to where they need to go. Invariably their train of thought goes something like this:

> *Where are you? Where are you going?*
> *Going from one place to another?*
> *Where are you? Where are you going?*
> *Returning home from vacation?*
> *Where are you? Where are you going?*

In all of these scenarios, the principle of the journey is quite simple: Know where you are, know where you are going, and plan the steps in-between.

Vision is a clear picture of a distant future built upon the foundation of intentionality and solidified by the successive realization of movements toward that future ...

Keeping your mind focused on this definition, let's go back

to a few questions posed earlier in the chapter: Where are you right now in your Faith walk? Where are you in your Kingdom work right now? Where are you in your relationship with Jesus? How are you doing in this vital relationship? Are you walking with God, chasing Him, or living in a peaceful state of co-existence? How close is your relationship with God right now? Do you embody the pursuit of God prescribed in Jeremiah 29:13 (NIV)? "You will seek me and find me when you seek me with all your heart." Are you fulfilling the first and greatest Commandment as defined by Jesus in Matthew 22:37-38 (NIV)? "Love the Lord your God with all your heart and with all your soul and with all your mind." Are you seeking Him with all your heart? Do you love Him with all of your heart, your mind and your soul? Where are you in your faith right now?

Another question that must be asked complements the driving directions and is a prerequisite for any journey worth taking. Now that we know where we are, we must determine where we are going. So, the logical question is: In your faith walk where are you going?

You know your strengths, you know your weaknesses, and you know the areas where you struggle even if no one else knows it. You also know your relationship with Jesus and you have some idea of where you are. You know *of* Him, do you *know* Him? You've read the Book, but does its message resonate in your soul? You may be able to quote chapter and verse, but is it written on your heart? Has your capacity for love grown as your knowledge has grown? What do you want your faith walk to look like this time next year? How about five years from now? Ten years from now? What do you want to accomplish in your faith walk before you die? Where are you going?

PERSONAL REFLECTIONS

———————————◾———————————

Vision is a clear picture of a distant future built upon the foundation of intentionality and solidified by the successive realization of movements toward that future.

In your faith walk, consider this definition of vision and the questions that follow:

In your faith walk, what do you want the future to look like ...

Next year:

Five years from now:

Fifteen years from now:

Before you die:

What steps do you need to take to intentionally walk toward that vision?

How will you know every day, week, or month that you are moving toward that vision? How can you measure your progress?

Who do you trust to monitor your progress by asking you these questions?

How are you doing on your progress toward your faith vision?

How is your focus on what you want to do in this critical area of your life?

What have you learned in your faith walk recently?

What is your greatest faith struggle right now?

What is your greatest faith joy right now?

I believe the questions in this exercise are absolutely critical to prepare you for a successful faith journey. How can you get there if you don't know where "there" is? How can you get there if you don't know where you are starting? How can you get there if you don't use tools, people, prayer and your vision to see if you are on track? How can you get there if you don't periodically stop the noise long enough to see if you are really living on purpose, to see if you are really living intentionally, to see if you are really living the abundant life?

VISION AND FAMILY

Where are you in your Family walk right now? Is everything as you would like it to be? How is your relationship with your son, your daughter, your husband, your wife? Is the family as close as it should be? Is there enough sharing of each other's lives or are you just a group of people living under the same roof? Is your spouse still your best friend? Do your children consider you one of their best friends and a trusted mentor?

Vision is a clear picture of a distant future built upon the foundation of intentionality and solidified by the successive realization of movements toward that future.

Let's continue by looking at the other side of the journey. What is your vision for your family? What do you want your family to look like and how do you want to interact with them one year from now? Five years from now? Ten years from now? Twenty-five years from now?

What do you want those who know you best to say about your marriage? What do you want your children to say about you and your spouse's relationship? What do you want your teen-aged children to say about you as a parent? When your children are grown, how do you want them to remember you as a parent? How do you hope they will describe you? How would you feel if they grew up to be just like you?

In the song *Cat's in the Cradle,* Harry Chapin proclaimed, "My boy was just like me. He had grown up just like me." But it was a statement of sadness, not celebration. In another ballad, Phillips, Craig, and Dean sing: "Lord I want to be just like you, 'cause he wants to be just like me. I want to be a holy example, for his innocent eyes to see. Let me be a living Bible, Lord, that

my little boy can read. I want to be just like yo
wants to be like me." Which song better reflec
right now? Which embodies your parenting?
you be singing?

There are so many questions involved i.. _
vision for your family and it is critical that we consider _
questions. So many people go through life hoping for the best
for their family, but fail to define what "the best" looks like. We
use coy phrases like "if you are going nowhere in particular
then you are sure to get there" to show our enlightenment. But
too often we do not have a plan for one of the most important
journeys of our own life – our family.

If I don't have an idea about what I want my marriage and
my relationship with my wife to look like, then I'm probably
not going to be intentionally moving toward anything. I would
just be marking time and hoping for the best. If I don't know
what specific values, lessons learned, and character traits that
I want to convey to my children before they leave my home,
then I'm certainly not going to do a good job of helping them
along the journey. Without meaning to, I would be leaving
them in the hands of anyone who might be more consistent
than me in their influence over one of the greatest gifts that
God has given me – my children.

This is simply not acceptable. We must have a vision. We
must have a plan for the growth, maturity, and Christ-
centered nature of our family as a whole, and for each
individual member. We are the ones that must make this plan
and put it into effect. Otherwise we just let this part of our
life be pulled with every ebb and flow, every shift of the tide.

PERSONAL REFLECTIONS

◼

Vision is a clear picture of a distant future built upon the foundation of intentionality and solidified by the successive realization of movements toward that future. In your family walk, consider this definition of vision and the questions that follow:

What do you want your family to look like in the following periods?

Next year:

Five years from now:

Fifteen years from now:

Before you die:

For each individual family member, record what you want the relationship to look like and what things you hope to do together – how you want to grow together – for the following periods:

Next year:

Five years from now:

Fifteen years from now:

Before you die:

For each individual family member, write down
those things that you really want to teach them.
Note things you wish you knew when you started
your life journey, or some critical lessons that you
learned and want to teach them during the periods
that follow:

Next year:

Five years from now:

Fifteen years from now:

Before you die:

For each of the visions mentioned above, what steps
do you need to take to intentionally walk toward
that vision?

For each of the visions mentioned above, how will
you know every day, week or month that you are
moving toward that vision? How can you measure
your progress?

Who do you know that you could trust to monitor your progress by asking you these questions?

How are you doing on your progress toward your family vision?

How is your focus on what you want to do in this critical area of your life?

What have you learned in your family walk recently?

What is your greatest family struggle right now?

What is your greatest family joy right now?

VISION AND VOCATION

How is your vocational vision right now? Where are you going to be five years from now? Ten years from now? Fifteen years from now? What will be the impact of the work that you do? Who will you be when you get where you are going? Do you have a vision for your vocation?

Vision is a clear picture of a distant future built upon the foundation of intentionality and solidified by the successive realization of movements toward that future.

So many people struggle with a vision for their vocation. We enter the workforce full of dreams and aspirations. Immediately our vision is tested against the backdrop of a cynical world. Pretty soon we lose our long range perspective and the view up close is blurry. We get so much "noise" thrown at us that we forget about our visions and our dreams. Then we forget how to dream. Sound familiar?

You may recognize this scenario as well: He works hard to achieve his heart's desires. He climbs the ladder of success day after day, year after year, and jumps through every important hoop for advancement. Sales excellence – got it. Team leader – got it. MBA – got it. Lead a larger organization – got it. Advancement, stock options, company car – got them. He knows where he is going and keeps getting affirmation that he is well along the road to his destination.

The problem comes when he arrives at that destination and asks himself: "Is this it?" His confusion is exacerbated when he realizes that all of the status, symbols and toys he has accumulated have left him empty and unfulfilled. To an envious observer, he has seemingly accomplished his dream. But in the presence of meaningless worldly possessions, power and position, he must learn to live with someone he has never truly known – himself.

Vocational visions can be incredibly deceiving and humbling. We can get duped into thinking that life is all about the next step or promotion. We get so caught up in it that it feels like life or death. All of a sudden we are passed over for the next promotion, and the next one, and the next one. We go from extreme vocational engagement to extreme vocational disassociation. Neither works, of course, and we're left with the task of finding our true selves.

Instead we must consider our vocation in the context of what God is trying to do in and through our lives. We must look at what we are now doing and want to do at work. We must ask how it relates to our God-ordained vision. Is there an element of our work that helps contribute to that vision? Does our career-planning take into account the impact we are supposed to have on the world?

How about you? Will the promotion you are seeking add to or take away from that impact? Will you still be in alignment with what God wants to do with your life? If you get the promotion will you be who you want to and should be by God's standards? What will it take to get there? Will the effort needed be a true reflection of who God wired you to be, or will masks be required?

These questions must be considered as you clarify the vision for the vocation that will routinely consume a large portion of your time and thoughts. Establishing a vision for your vocation is critical because in all areas of our life – Faith, Family, and Vocation – you must plan for the following: Where am I going? Who do I want to be when I get there? What impact do I want to have on this world?

Living the Abundant Life

PERSONAL REFLECTIONS

Vision is a clear picture of a distant future built upon the foundation of intentionality and solidified by the successive realization of movements toward that future. What do you want to be doing in your vocation in the following periods?

Next year:

Five years from now:

Fifteen years from now:

Before you die:

A true vision is a God-inspired vision. *As we get closer to making that vision a reality, we get closer to ourselves and to God.* Based on the previous sentence, do you think your vocational vision is a true one?

How does your vocation vision bring you closer to who you think God designed you to be; closer to what you were destined to do; closer to the impact you are supposed to have on this world?

What is your vision for your vocation? How will you know every day, week or month that you are moving toward that vision? How can you measure your progress?

Who do you know that you could trust to monitor your progress and ask you these questions?

How are you doing on your progress toward your vocation vision?

How is your focus on what you want to do in this critical area of your life?

What have you learned in your vocation recently?

What is your greatest vocation struggle right now?

What brings the greatest satisfaction in your
vocation right now?

Does your vocation feed your passion in some way?

Is God glorified by your vocation? How?

LIFE VISION

Life is composed of Faith, Family, and Vocation. Vision is
comprised of three elements – destination, ideal self, and
impact. Each of these elements must be employed in our
vision and our visions must include our Faith, Family, and
Vocation walks. To have a vision for one area and not another
creates an imbalance that can and must be dealt with sooner
or later.

But life cannot be separated too neatly into different
compartments. If we try to make our Faith, Family, and
Vocation walks separate and distinct journeys, we will fail.
These paths are blended together in such a fashion that what
occurs in one always affects the others in some manner. We
must have a vision for our Faith, Family, and Vocation, but there
is a bigger picture that we must consider lest we slice life too
finely – we must develop a God-ordained vision for our lives.

Vision is a clear picture of a distant future built upon the foundation of intentionality and solidified by the successive realization of movements toward that future.

In the big scheme of things, why are you here and where are you going? Why did God put you on the face of the earth? Who did He make you to be? What impact does God want to have on the world through you? These are questions all of us must ask when we start considering our life vision. When we finish with the self-analysis, the introspection that comes from dissecting our Faith, Family, and Vocation, we are left with our relationship with God. We must then ask Him the question: Why am I here?

In Chapter 3, we concluded that Passion is the first element of abundance. With passion comes the focus and determination necessary for achieving the purpose God put on your heart. A life vision works *out* what passion has worked *in*. A life vision takes those things that are in your heart and identifies what you are supposed to do with them.

A life Vision will differ dramatically from one person to the next. As I considered my Passion (leadership; connecting with and lifting people) and my Burden (the lack of victory, joy and significance in the life of God's children) I was left to wonder where it was all supposed to lead. I knew what was on my heart and its connection to God, but I struggled with what I would do with this knowledge. What I discovered was the Vision for my life as a whole. I realized that my Vision was "children of the King living out their John 10:10 inheritance." Let's examine that statement for some of the critical components of every vision – destination, ideal self, and impact.

First, my Vision has nothing to do with *me* achieving something. We often get so focused on ourselves that we fail to notice those around us. We fail to realize our impact on others. We neglect the Impact component of our Vision. I grew weary of all the visions that had me in the center of the circle. I finally realized that if my vision were all about me I would never satisfy my innate need to impact the world around me. Thus, my Vision is all about other people. It is other-directed.

My entire focus is helping as many people as I can live their John 10:10 inheritance.

Second, destination and ideal self flow from the heavy emphasis on abundance and impact. My exact destination is not so important as long as what I am doing helps children of the King live out their John 10:10 inheritance. My life vision is oriented around helping others live the abundant life that Jesus came for them to have. If I'm doing that, I'm *there*. If I'm not doing that, I've missed my destination. In order to live out the destination component of my vision, I must commit a portion of each day to doing something that helps others live the abundant life Jesus promised they could have.

When I help others live abundant lives – at work, at home, at church - I am who I was intended to be. My ideal self doesn't require that I wait ten years to achieve something or gain some title. When I work hard to increase the "abundance quotient" in the world then I am living out my life Vision.

Finally, my overall life Vision keeps me from getting "lost in the weeds" when it comes to the individual visions for my life – Faith, Family and Vocation. A life vision will integrate all of these components. It ensures that all of our pursuits, in all areas of life, are reflective of the purpose for which God has called us. A life Vision functions as an umbrella, of sorts, under which all of our visions are sheltered and strengthened. Thus, our Faith, Family, and Vocation visions must come from and contribute to our life vision.

As a Christ follower, a growing relationship with Jesus must be the overriding goal in my life. My Faith walk must be oriented around this goal, but the vision for my Faith comes from and contributes to my life Vision of "children of the King living out their John 10:10 inheritance." Likewise, there are many things I want and need to experience with my Family. But all of those things, all of the visions for my Family, must be oriented around the life Vision that God put on my heart. I must first contribute to my family living abundant lives as children of the King.

Also, my vocational vision may include goals related to career position, professional influence, and financial matters.

But all of those goals must be oriented around and contribute to the life vision. My co-workers are children of the King, and they, too, should be aware of their esteemed position and the abundant life that should be theirs. Our life Vision must be at the core of all the visions in our Faith, Family, and Vocation. That way every journey, path, and walk we take will be governed by and contribute to the success of our life Vision.

My Vision may seem somewhat esoteric, and is admittedly very broad. Yours may not be. The important thing is that your Vision be actionable and reflective of what God is calling you to do with your life. Your Vision should serve as a reminder of why you were put on the face of the earth, where you are going, who you want to be when you get there, and what impact you want to and are supposed to have by virtue of your being alive.

PERSONAL REFLECTIONS

Vision is a clear picture of a distant future built upon the foundation of intentionality and solidified by the successive realization of movements toward that future. A true vision is a God-inspired vision. As we zero in on making that vision a reality, we get closer to ourselves and to God. Spend some quality time with the following questions:

What is the most important thing that you are supposed to do with your life?

Living the Abundant Life

What do you see when you think of a tomorrow that is better than today? What is your role in that tomorrow?

What is the destination that you have been tapped on the shoulder by God to strive for?

Who are you supposed to be when you get there?

What is your Ideal Self?

What impact are you supposed to have on the world?

What is your God-ordained Vision?

How will you know every day, week or month that you are moving toward your life Vision? How can you measure your progress?

Who do you know that you could trust to monitor your progress and ask you these questions?

How clear is your life Vision?

How is your focus on this critical area of your life?

What have you learned in your journey recently?

What is your greatest struggle in this journey right now?

How is your vision influencing your actions right now?

How is your life vision feeding your passion?

How is God being glorified by your life vision?

PLANE GUARD AND VISION

As a Surface Warfare and Bridge Watch Officer, I spent a great deal of time on the bridge of a guided missile destroyer. I was fortunate because I absolutely loved what I was doing and never grew tired of even the most mundane operations at sea. There was something about using 125,000 rumbling shaft horsepower that made my job always feel fresh!

Occasionally we were called on to perform a very taxing evolution called Plane Guard. This entailed following an aircraft carrier at a distance of between 2,000-4,000 yards. The goal was to be prepared to rescue any pilots or airmen who went overboard. The danger in this evolution came from following the carrier so closely.

Carriers have a nautical edge called "the law of gross tonnage." This means they generally do not worry about smaller ships. They let smaller ships worry about them. Consequently, carriers sometimes fail to let smaller vessels know when they are changing course or speed. This is a problem because carriers are always changing course and speed while looking for different wind envelopes in order to launch their aircraft. As the plane guard we had to be in position whether they told us what they were doing or not.

As a result of this uncertainty, we had a hard and fast rule when we were operating in the vicinity of an aircraft carrier. An Officer on the bridge-watch team always had to have his eyes on that carrier. Never, not even for a second, would you permit that big thing to slip away from your gaze. Forget manners. For example, if I asked the Officer who was watching the carrier where it was, he would not look at me when he answered the question – nor did I want him to! My only requirements were for him to point to the beast, give me distance in yards, and tell me if we were opening or closing in distance. Under no circumstances did I want him to look at me while he was on watch.

This approach may seem somewhat obsessive-compulsive unless you consider the alternative. I served on a different ship that was an incredible fighting machine. Four years after I left the ship news broke that it had run into a carrier. Fortunately no one was killed but the bow of the ship was destroyed and several million dollars worth of damage was done. People were fired, careers were lost, all because someone momentarily forgot about a vessel large enough to carry 100 fixed-wing aircraft and over 6,000 people.

How do you lose sight of an aircraft carrier? How do you forget it's there? What in the world can possibly distract your attention from keeping such a massive ship in view when you are operating in the vicinity of it? I don't know the answer to those questions. Perhaps it's much like the answer we would give when asked how we can possibly lose sight of a vision that God placed on our heart. Despite being tapped on the shoulder by God, who wants us to do something for Him, we frequently lose sight of our purpose. It doesn't make sense, but we sometimes lose our perspective.

On a ship, you must always have someone with eyes on the carrier. Not to do so would invite a tragedy of immense proportions – dramatic loss of life could result. In our life, we must always keep our eyes on the vision that God has placed on our hearts. There are so many things that can distract us, things that seem logical at the time. But the result of these things taking the place of our God-ordained vision can be tragic. Created in His image He wants us to live an abundant life. One life lost, one life lived in spiritual squalor, one life squandered because no one was watching the vision, is also a dramatic loss of life.

I like to tell people that as a Naval Officer making a grievous mistake like running into a carrier "can ruin your day." Likewise, losing sight of your God-ordained vision can literally ruin your life. When ships fail dramatically, they sometimes hit each other. When we fail dramatically with our God-ordained vision, we just simply drift apart. We go in one direction, our God-ordained vision goes in the other. As James said in a different context so many years ago, "My brothers, this should not be" (Jas 3:10 NIV).

Living the Abundant Life

VISION AND PASSION

Passion is the first element of abundance. There is power
in determining what the hand of God has placed on your heart
to care deeply about. Passion must be anchored by a burden
that represents the cross that we bear. It is the necessary
compass that always points us, our actions, our motives and
our passions toward God.

Vision is the second element of abundance. Vision ensures
that we are living on purpose. Having a vision means we are
moving intentionally toward something and that our life has a
purpose larger than daily circumstances. Vision helps us keep
a proper perspective on today by constantly placing it in the
context of tomorrow. A God-inspired vision helps us exclaim,
"Today may not have been as I would have designed it, but I
moved closer to the tomorrow that I am seeking and that God

wants me to pursue. It was a great day!" That is the impact of a life vision on our daily existence.

In science, hydrogen is an important element and oxygen is obviously necessary to sustain life. Individually both of these elements are of great value. But combining them gives us a product that is, at the same time, different, necessary, and useful. It may also be the most powerful force in nature. The water that results from combining two parts hydrogen with one part oxygen sustains life and has many uses that range from survival, hygiene and entertainment. The list is virtually endless. Hydrogen and oxygen are both useful and necessary, but are much more powerful when combined as water.

Likewise passion and vision are useful individually and necessary for abundance. You cannot have abundance without either. But the impact of both is magnified exponentially when they are combined. You know your passion and it lights you on fire. You know the burden which keeps your passion focused on a Godly source and Godly purposes. You are "burning" the right way. You determine your life vision and strive every day to move closer to the fulfillment of that vision.

To be on the road to abundance, though, you must ensure that your passion is related to your vision. You must look at your overall life vision and those visions for your Faith, Family, and Vocation. Then you must identify the role passion plays in those visions. Your passion represents your heart and must be integrated into those visions. Too many people identify a vision, but fail to take into account what God put on their heart to do. They may feel stimulated for a while, caught up in the excitement of pursuing a goal, but the emptiness always returns if that vision was not formed from our passion and our passion from God.

So, when identifying your vision, ask yourself what the vision you are discerning has to do with the passion God put on your heart. In doing this you will ensure that your vision is always related to the passion God put on your heart and the burden He wants to use to keep you anchored to Him. In other words, the destination, ideal self and impact will all be related to both the passion and burden which are at the core of who we are.

Living the Abundant Life

Vision is a clear picture of a distant future built upon the foundation of intentionality and solidified by the successive realization of movements toward that future.

Vision works out what passion works in and keeps us focused on achieving tomorrow what God put in our heart yesterday. In the next chapter we will continue the journey toward abundance and look at the tools God has given us to accomplish this work.

PERSONAL REFLECTIONS

What is your God-inspired passion?

What is your God-appointed burden?

What is your God-ordained life vision?

How is your life vision related to the passion and burden God placed on your heart?

What is your vision for your faith? How is it related to your life vision?

What is your vision for you family? How is it related to your life vision?

What is your vision for your vocation? How is it related to your life vision?

5

G I F T S

"The truth is not that God is finding us a place for our gifts but that God has created us and our gifts for a place of his choosing – and we will only be ourselves when we are finally there." [1]

Passion is the first element of abundance. It represents what God placed on your heart to care so deeply about. When passion comes we realize what it is that makes time stand still and all else fade away. Our pulse is elevated and little else matters. This passion must be anchored by a glorious burden that keeps it constantly pointed to our hearts innermost and truest desire – God. Burden keeps passion focused on God and is the cross we are to bear.

Vision is the second element of abundance. Our life vision works out what passion has worked in. It takes what is in your heart and tells you where you are to go with it. It identifies a distant future and helps you see with more clarity exactly how that future is going to look. With a life vision in place we live intentionally, focused on a distant future while making steps daily toward that future. This successive realization ensures that we are striving toward the God-ordained vision that will make our life count.

Jesus came so we might live the abundant life. Passion and vision combine to make a powerful difference in our life and in our quest for abundance. But as powerful as passion and vision are there is something missing. The missing element essentially deals with the gap between our passion, which fills our life today, and our vision, which is about a distant future.

The gap between today and tomorrow can rob us of the journey to abundance that we started when we discovered our passion, burden, and vision.

The third element of abundance helps fill this gap. The third element you need to live the abundant life is an understanding of your spiritual gifts. Spiritual gifts are those abilities that we are given by God in order to do the work He has put us here to do. He gave us the heart to do something (passion); He gave us an image of what we are to do (vision); and He gave us the tools of our trade in order to carry out the plan (gifts). That is where gifts fit in the journey toward abundance. We will delve deeper into gifts in a moment. For now though, envision a couple of scenarios that I hope will help you see the need for an understanding of gifts in order to live the abundant life.

WORKING OUTSIDE THE REALM OF OUR GIFTEDNESS

I remember watching a peer of mine go through a very difficult period. He was a star performer in a company and had advanced rapidly. His strengths were in operations. There was nothing that he loved more than to bring order out of chaos, to put processes and systems in place where there were none or where existing structures no longer worked. He thrived in this type of situation and was able to apply the same solution to every process he touched. He would find the problem, blow it up, place a process on top of the new structure, micro-manage it, chart the results, and celebrate the improvements. He was very successful at what he did.

Then a big problem occurred – he was promoted. Unfortunately, he was not promoted into a position where he would be managing the same process. He was promoted to a position that had some processes to improve, but his new position required consummate people skills. It required that he lead people and teach them to lead others. He was expected to engage people's hearts, get them to buy into his vision, and coach them toward assuming more responsibility.

I want to use the terms passion and vision loosely to emphasize a point. The young manager I'm talking about had plenty of passion for processes and for dramatically improving poor performance standards. There was no weakness in his vision, since he could envision extraordinary improvements in the systems and processes he established.

Unfortunately, that is not what happened. People started using the new processes and they applied his common sense strategies, but they began to resent him because every single performance blip resulted in yet another spreadsheet or report. Their enthusiasm, energy, and entrepreneurial spirit were choked by the burden of the processes they were required to follow. Consequently he started losing people – the wrong people. The poor performers remained. They just filed the reports and did what was required to keep their job. The ones that left were the good ones, the ones who could produce results, but needed some ownership of both the results and the processes. They left in droves.

He had passion, vision, and a proven track record. The problem was this gentleman did not have the gifts he needed in order to run an organization that was incredibly leadership intensive. This guy was the perfect candidate to manage an operation after you have gotten it started. But putting him in a major leadership role that required dramatic cultural change and the constant development of human potential placed him squarely outside of his gift set. He was simply not wired for what he was required to do.

The "Peter principle" suggests that people tend to rise to their relative level of incompetence.[2] They work their way through the ranks by doing things they do well at and frequently don't stop getting promoted until they are unfortunate enough to manage something they are simply not wired to do. They reach their relative level of incompetence.

Anyone who has seen the movie *Heartbreak Ridge,* with Clint Eastwood, has seen this principle in action. In the movie, Gunnery Sergeant Highway (Eastwood) was pitted against a

Major who had recently transferred from Supply to Infantry. For those of you who are not as familiar with the different jobs within the military let me assure you that the Supply Corps, while necessary for any military operation, is not generally known for its acts of heroism and bravery. So this Supply Officer – very successful in his field – transferred to Infantry and immediately felt he could command a field operation. We all waited through the entire movie for "Gunney Highway" to save the day and put the Major in his place. If you saw the movie, you will recall it did happen. Gunney Highway was vindicated on the top of a hill in Grenada while the Major was exposed as the living embodiment of the "Peter Principle." He had risen to his relative level of incompetence!

In the case of my peer, he was an incredibly gifted manager and administrator, but was not personally equipped for the type of leadership required by his position. Did that mean he could not do the job? That question could be hotly debated. But the fact is that he could not personally do those aspects of his job that were the most critical for success. For him to be successful, he needed someone in his organization who could dramatically strengthen his people development shortcomings which would have in turn leveraged his operational strengths.

His passion was great. His vision was clear. But his gifts were ill-matched with the role he was assigned. As good a guy as he was he could not give what he did not have. He could not use skill sets and attributes that he did not posses.

For those of you who are familiar with spiritual gifts, I ask that you not pre-judge this section based on the above example. We will get to the Biblical basis of gifts, how they are conveyed and how they are applied shortly. When we consider them, I will also address what I believe to be a damaging interpretation of the use and application of spiritual gifts.

Let me further illustrate gifts with a more faith-based example. Bob is a businessman whose life has taken a dramatic turn over the last several years. Ten years ago he started his own company after a very successful tenure as an executive with a large corporation. Bob immediately grew his company into a strong and profitable organization. After five years he achieved every financial goal he had set and looked forward to a bright future.

Amidst all of the fan fare Bob knew something was missing. He had a growing awareness of the emptiness inside. Bob and his wife had attended church together for their entire marriage, but he was never really involved like she was. He went because he was expected to and because the contacts were good for his business. But there came a time when Bob knew that he was no longer going just for the contacts. He was going because he needed meaning in his life. His business no longer provided the fulfillment he needed.

After struggling with this emptiness, he met with some close friends and his pastor. Eventually, he was led by these people and the Holy Spirit into a personal relationship with Jesus. This absolutely transformed his life and provided the meaning he was so sorely missing.

Bob's view of his work changed even more as he matured in his faith. He began to look forward to church and church-related activities. He studied his Bible every night and enjoyed the constant growth in his knowledge of and relationship with Jesus. People responded well to him in small study groups and he led several such groups successfully. Eventually Bob concluded that, because of his new relationship with Jesus and his passion for his faith, he should shift into full-time ministry. He sold his company, went to seminary, and within three years became the pastor at a small church.

A strange thing happened, though, after Bob became the pastor. It took a couple of years, but he gradually became aware that he no longer enjoyed his role as a pastor. In fact, he didn't enjoy going to church or reading his Bible. What's more, he didn't have the relationship with Jesus that he had before he became a pastor.

Bob had a passion for helping change lives. He had a real burden for people living under the illusion that worldly success equated to life success. He knew he wanted to be a part of changing that. He had a vision for everyone, particularly business people like himself and he wanted them to understand what a personal relationship with Jesus was all about.

What Bob did not realize was that his gift set made him better suited for other roles than being a pastor. He had the gift of leadership, so when he was faced with a growing faith walk, he wanted to become the symbol of the ultimate faith walk – a pastor. Instead, he should have looked at his passion, his vision, *and* his gift set (not to mention large quantities of prayer!) to help determine what the next step should be.

Unsuited for his role as a pastor, Bob was gifted in other ways that complimented both the work he did in the church and the work he did in his business – administration, leadership, and giving in particular. There was nothing about Bob's passion, burden, or vision that required he perform in the role of pastor. He could have fulfilled his passion, burden, and vision by doing his work for God in a corporate setting. And because he had been blessed with the ability to amass large quantities of personal wealth he could have used those funds to multiply his efforts for the King.

In the end God may have been better served if Bob would have stayed with his company and acted on his passion, burden, and vision in a manner that fully exercised the spiritual gifts he had been given. This would have saved him from trying to do Kingdom work with gifts that he just did not possess.

AN ALIGNED LIFE — BILL BRIGHT

You may remember our earlier discussion of Bill Bright. As the late founder of Campus Crusade for Christ, he had a "gift experience" that was the direct opposite of Bob's. Specifically, he reminds me of what it looks like to have your passion, burden, vision and gifts aligned for maximum Kingdom impact and abundant living.

At a relatively young age, Bill Bright narrowed down his passion, burden and vision. He even went so far as to put a candle on a globe and claim the world for Christ. But, he did not try to preach his way into converting the world to Christ. Bill Bright was an economics major with a minor in sociology, who let Jesus grab hold of his life and do amazing things through him. And, like Bob, Bill Bright was not gifted to be a pastor.

Instead he founded an amazing organization that, in 2002, had "25,000 full-time staff and over 553,000 trained volunteer staff in 196 countries in areas representing 99.6 percent of the world's population."[3] His Campus Crusade for Christ produced the Jesus Video which is touted as the "most widely viewed film ever produced. It has been translated into more than 730 languages and viewed by more than 4.5 billion people in 234 countries. More than 148 million people have indicated making salvation decisions for Christ after viewing it live."

It is amazing when you consider the impact that Jesus had and is having through Bill Bright and the organization he founded. I would propose that despite his intelligence, despite his ability to run a large organization, despite his close walk with Jesus, Bill Bright would not have accomplished nearly what he did had he worked outside of his gift set. He responded to a calling and did it in a manner that was consistent with who God wired him to be. Passion, burden, vision and gifts were all working in unison with the way God intended them to be used.

ALIGNMENT IN THE FAMILY

I still remember some of the discussions my wife, Beth, and I used to have. They were usually after a period when I had obsessed over finances and unintentionally made her feel self-conscious of her role as a stay-at-home mother. Sometimes a question from someone about when she was going "back to work" and use her degree (elementary education) would initiate the conversation. Other times it would be comments by her peers that made it sound like a motivational deficit because she chose to stay at home with her children instead of having a "real job" earning a real income. The source varied but the result was consistent – an incredibly uncomfortable situation for our family.

During the ensuing conversations with Beth I would emphasize my desire for our children's well being ahead of everything else, thus offering support for her decision to stay home. However, in the next breath, I would openly admit that I looked forward to the day when she could return to work.

Little did I know that I unintentionally, and unfairly, burdened her with guilt when I spoke of her return to employment in such glowing terms. We had been a military family first and then a corporate one when I left the service. Our first, then second, then third child came as we were climbing the proverbial corporate ladder, and excess funds were hard to come by. Admittedly, I did get an extra bounce in my step when I considered a second income for our family.

Fortunately for us, and especially for our children, we never wavered from the decision to put our children ahead of our finances. More accurately, Beth never wavered in her commitment to the lifestyle we had chosen. Despite the sometimes bleak financial picture; despite the occasional, usually unintentional hurtful comments by others; despite her own concerns that she was not making the most use of her education; she stayed the course and stayed at home with our children.

Beth used her gifts in a manner consistent with her vision for her family and for her own sense of purpose. She could easily have returned to teaching and there would have been nothing wrong with that. But there was something inside of her that would not let her be at peace with that course of action. She had to stay at home and teach our children full-time, in what was perhaps the most formative period of their lives.

She was there to fully express her love for our children. She was there to pour her life into theirs. She was there to teach them joy through the radiance from her own life. She was there to help them understand painful times or just hold them until the pain subsided. She was there to ensure that the message of Jesus Christ was placed in their hearts. She was there to ensure that He was truly a part of their life, not just their weekend. She was there to take them to school, to pick them up from school, to take them to the park, to go on field trips with them, to enroll them in gymnastics, and theatre, and t-ball, and soccer, and everything else that you can imagine. She was there.

Beth is an incredibly gifted and talented woman with a

Living the Abundant Life

wonderful heart for people in general and for children in particular. She could have used her gifts in many ways, but she listened to that passion, that burden, that vision inside of her and chose the path that was proper at the time. She chose to live in true alignment with one of the most important visions of her life and used her God-given gifts for her children first. There will come a time when she will have to turn those gifts, that passion and that vision in a different direction – children grow up and they move on. But she kept "first things first" and stayed in alignment with her calling – and was absolutely beautiful, inside and out, as she did so.

PERSONAL REFLECTIONS

How does it feel on those occasions when what you are gifted at is aligned with what you are doing in your Faith, Family, or Vocation?

How does it feel when you find yourself spending most of your time in an area in which your capacity or interest level is not strong, or misaligned?

THE NEED FOR GIFTS

Spiritual gifts are the third element of abundance. You can know your passion and be on the road to abundance. You can have a clear picture of your vision and start making the trip. But in order to approach the pinnacle you must get into the details about what role you are to play in making your vision come true. You do this by understanding what your gifts are. As you discover your gifts, you will understand more clearly what your role is in making your vision a reality.

Let me rephrase that for impact. Having clarity about your vision – what you are to bring about in your Faith, Family, and Vocation – does not necessarily mean that you have clarity about the role you are to play in bringing that vision to fruition. Some people mistake having a vision with having an understanding of their role in the vision. Don't make that mistake.

A vision for my Vocation might include building an organization that continuously grows the people in the organization. The leadership development component of building this type of organization is perfectly suited for both my vision and my gift set. However, the administration component – where we are continuously aware of who we are developing, what stage of development they are in, what needs remain to maximize their growth, and scheduling those next steps – is an area in which I am not gifted by God. The vision is mine, but I need someone with other gifts to turn my vision into reality.

A vision for your Family might include developing certain characteristics or attributes in your children. You may be well-suited, gifted, for teaching and developing some of those attributes, but not particularly well-suited for others. The critical nature of this vision may require that you work with your spouse to develop a plan that will use his or her gifts where yours might not be strong enough to accomplish the vision. Again, the vision is yours, but you need someone else to help make the vision a reality.

It may be your vision, but that does not mean that you are the only one involved in bringing the vision to life. In fact, if it is a God-ordained vision there is little likelihood that you will be able to make it happen by yourself. You will need to get other people involved and will likely need people with different gifts than you in order to bring the vision to fruition.

Know your passion, know your burden, know your vision, and understand your gifts. Through an understanding of these elements of abundance and how they work together we can come to understand our own journey to abundance. As we continue along that journey let us take a closer look at spiritual gifts.

WHAT ARE SPIRITUAL GIFTS?

C. Peter Wagner uses the following definition of a spiritual gift: "A spiritual gift is a special attribute given by the Holy Spirit to every member of the Body of Christ, according to God's grace, for use within the context of the Body."[4]

As we enter the discussion of what gifts are and where they come from I want to share several Biblical passages, not opinion, as to the origin of the concept and reality of spiritual gifts. After the Bible references I will point out a few items then move to the next reference. Then we will look at the overall interpretation of what we have read together.

1 Corinthians 12:1-7 (NLT): *And now, dear brothers and sisters, I will write about the special abilities the Holy Spirit gives to each of us...Now there are different kinds of spiritual gifts, but it is the same Holy Spirit who is the source of them all. There are different kinds of service in the church, but it is the same God who does the work through all of us. A spiritual gift is given to each of us as a means of helping the entire church.*

These "special abilities" or gifts are given by the Holy Spirit. This means that the gifts are conveyed to those in relationship with Jesus. If you are born again – in relationship with Jesus – you receive the Holy Spirit. If you receive the Holy Spirit, a spiritual gift – at least one – is given to you.

Romans 12:4-5 (NLT): *Just as our bodies have many parts and each part has a special function, so it is with Christ's body. We are all parts of his one body, and each of us has different work to do. And since we are all one body in Christ, we belong to each other, and each of us needs all the others.*

Romans 12:6-8 (NIV): *We have different gifts, according to the grace given us. If a man's gift is prophesying, let him use it in proportion to his faith. If it is serving, let him serve; if it is teaching, let him teach; if it is encouraging, let him encourage; if it is contributing to the needs of others, let him give generously; if it is leadership, let him govern diligently; if it is showing mercy, let him do it cheerfully.*

The Bible draws the analogy between all of the parts of the body working together to function effectively and the body of Christ working in a similar manner. Paul points out that just as the body parts need each other so are we dependent on one another. Each of us has at least one gift. Our gifts are given by God and are to be used to fulfill His purposes for our life. Using our specific gifts will complement the work being done by others who are using their gifts. "We are all parts of his one body, and each of us has different work to do. And since we are all one body in Christ, we belong to each other, and each of us needs all the others." If we have been given the gift of teaching? "Let him teach." Given the gift of serving? "Let him serve." Given the gift of leadership? "Let him govern diligently." We have all been given gifts and are instructed to use those gifts.

1 Corinthians 12:12-27 (NLT): *The human body has many parts, but the many parts make up only one body. So it is with the body of Christ ... But God made our bodies with many parts, and he has put each part just where he wants It ... Yes, there are many parts, but only one body. The eye can never say to the hand, "I don't need you." The head can't say to the feet, "I don't need you."... Now all of you together are Christ's*

Living the Abundant Life

body, and each one of you is a separate and necessary part of it.

Ephesians 4:4-8 (NLT): *We are all on body, we have the same Spirit, and we have all been called to the same glorious future. There is only one Lord, one faith, one baptism, and there is only one God and Father, who is over us all and in us all and living through us all. However, he has given each one of us a special gift according to the generosity of Christ …*

Again the emphasis is on the body and the similarity between the parts of the body (both complimentary and necessary) and those of us in the body of Christ. When the Bible says "each one of you is a separate and necessary part of "the body of Christ" it is an awe-inspiring message. We are not an afterthought, not a piece that may or may not fit. We are an integral part of the plan. We are a "necessary part of it."

1 Peter 4:10-11 (NLT): *God has given gifts to each of you from his great variety of spiritual gifts. Manage them well so that God's generosity can flow through you. Are you called to be a speaker? Then speak as though God himself were speaking through you. Are you called to help others? Do it with all the strength and energy that God supplies. Then God will be given glory in everything through Jesus Christ.*

To paraphrase the apostle, God has given gifts to each of us from His great storehouse of spiritual gifts. Manage them well so that His generosity can flow through you. To manage anything, you must first gain an in-depth awareness and understanding of whatever it is that you desire to manage. What are the variables that you are seeking to alter? What are you trying to minimize and what do you seek to maximize? What will success and failure look like?

To manage indicates that you will coordinate the activities of something in order to achieve the maximum efficiency and results of that something. It logically follows that if you do not know or understand the details of whatever it is that you are trying to manage, then you cannot effectively manage the process. Thus, you cannot possibly achieve the desired results.

The Bible tells us that we have been given gifts directly from God and that we are to manage them. It is God's desire that we manage the gifts He has given us, use them to their fullest potential, and use them for His purposes. In doing so His generosity may flow through us.

A failure to be aware of our gifts, manage them, or employ them properly can stop the flow of God's generosity. Take note of that. God wants to let His generosity flow through us and into the world so we can do our part to achieve His purposes. When we fail to use the gifts He has given us, we effectively cut off this flow. We may be working and even working hard, but that does not necessarily mean we are doing Kingdom work.

Can we possibly model the abundance that Jesus promised if we don't spend our life using the gifts that the Holy Spirit grants to us? The hand of God gives us these things – can there be any question that we are intended to use them?

GIFTS AND NATURAL ABILITIES

Spiritual gifts are given to those in relationship with Jesus by the Holy Spirit. However, there is a difference between these gifts and natural abilities. This is an important distinction, because we can be duped into thinking that our natural abilities represent what we are to do with our life. Such thinking may result in some degree of success, but it will not propel us toward abundant living.

For example, when I left my hometown at 18 years of age and joined the Navy I developed an ability to focus that was sorely lacking when I was in high school. All of the sudden I started excelling in academic pursuits where before, calling me mediocre would have been generous! In the service, I developed the attitude that there was nothing I could not do if I worked hard and long enough. I was always willing to put the extra hours in and had full confidence in my ability to "get it" if I studied long enough.

Because of this mindset, I was able to do a number of things very well. I became an excellent communications operator with a particular strength in shipboard satellite and high frequency communications. As an officer I won a ship handling award, was strong in communications, and excelled in an area in which I had been previously intimidated. My ability to focus led to the ability to develop strength in a multitude of areas. However, that did not mean those were my areas of giftedness or that they represented concentrations I should commit my life to.

Just because you are good at something does not mean that you are supposed to spend your life doing it. Just because you have developed the ability to make large sums of money does not mean that you are wired to do it for the rest of your life. Quite frankly, it is not hard to be good at something.

We often tell our children the maxim of Stonewall Jackson: "You can be whatever you resolve to be."[5] In many ways that maxim is true. Once we commit ourselves to something, we can usually make it happen. A full resolve is often the pathway to success.

Gifts are different. Abundance is different. What we are seeking is what God resolved that we should be. What we are looking for is our role in the Kingdom work that we have been called to do. Our resolve is transformed from finding things that we are good at – things we can generally accomplish without God's intervention – to finding those things that God wired us to be and to do.

Though being good at something does not always mean you are specifically gifted in an area, natural abilities may be indications of spiritual gifts. However, there is an important caveat. If someone has always had the ability to comfort others in need or lift their spirits but he or she is not in relationship with Jesus, does he or she have the spiritual gifts of mercy or encouragement?

No, they do not. We receive the Holy Spirit when we are born again and "it is the one and only Holy Spirit who distributes these gifts" (1 Cor 12:11 NLT). By definition then the propensity that the individual is showing is not a spiritual gift. This propensity, this natural ability, if you will, can be an indication of the area of giftedness that God wants to bestow upon us and use us for in this world. Billy Graham had this to say about this topic:

> *It appears that God can take a talent and transform it by the power of the Holy Spirit and use it as a spiritual gift. In fact, the difference between a spiritual gift and a natural talent is frequently a cause for speculation by many people. I am not sure we can always draw a sharp line between spiritual gifts and natural abilities – both of which, remember, come ultimately from God.*[6]

Leaders lead. Creative communicators may do amazing things with art. Givers are generous of their time and resources. Teachers teach. All of these can occur before people develop a relationship with Jesus. It can happen before they are born again and receive the Holy Spirit. Although the gifts may not have been fully bestowed, there may be natural abilities in place that serve as precursors of what could and should develop in that person's life. These natural abilities may therefore represent a diamond in the rough, waiting for the infusion of the Holy Spirit to develop into the mature spiritual gift that will glorify God and help in the journey to abundance.

Living the Abundant Life

PERSONAL REFLECTIONS

■

In what areas do you have strong natural abilities?

What types of activities or interests do you find yourself naturally gravitating toward?

What skills or attributes are in common when you are doing those activities?

Why is it important for you to know your spiritual Gifts?

Why does the Bible say that it is important for you to know your spiritual Gifts? Who does the Bible say is given at least one spiritual Gift?

Are you living in relationship with Jesus?

Do you have at least one spiritual Gift given to you
by the Holy Spirit?

WHY ARE SPIRITUAL GIFTS NOT EMPHASIZED MORE?

Spiritual gifts are given to each person who is in relationship with Jesus. They are conveyed from the Holy Spirit and are the implements of our Ephesians 2:10 (NIV) – "we are God's workmanship, created in Christ Jesus to do good works, which God prepared in advance for us to do" – journey. If the Bible is so clear on spiritual gifts, why don't we hear more about them? I propose there are several reasons for the lack of emphasis on spiritual gifts.

Spiritual Gifts Have Been Left to Charismatics

A broad misunderstanding of spiritual gifts has led some to believe that they are entirely about speaking in tongues, interpreting tongues, healing and miracles. This has led some to conclude that spiritual gifts belong only in the charismatic movement.

Let there be no misunderstanding. Speaking in tongues, interpreting tongues and healing, are all mentioned in the Bible and are indeed spiritual gifts. There is a great deal of debate about which gifts are prevalent in the world today. Are people still healed today as they were 2000 years ago? I simply do not know or intend to enter the debate.

I do know this. You and I and anyone else who is in

relationship with Jesus has been given at least one spiritual gift. I also know that God does not give anything by accident or without intent. We are given gifts, we are supposed to know what they are, and we are supposed to "manage them well so that God's generosity can flow through us." Our failure to do so is the equivalent of saying "no thank you" to God for the gift He has bestowed.

Spiritual Gifts Have Not Been Taught

I went to church regularly in my youth, but do not remember learning about spiritual gifts. I had no idea what they were. Even as a "mature" Christian I was not taught about spiritual gifts. I constantly meet seemingly mature Christians who do not have a good idea of what spiritual gifts are. I believe there continues to be truth in what Billy Graham wrote in 1978: "Every believer has at least one gift from the Holy Spirit. A weakness in today's churches is the failure to recognize, cultivate, and use fully the gifts God has given people in the pews."[7]

The findings from several surveys highlight the lack of knowledge about spiritual gifts. This lack of knowledge is especially alarming because the Bible is so very clear about them. In their news release announcing the results of their survey, the Barna Research Group documented the following:[8]

Among born again adults, the percentage that say they have heard of spiritual gifts but do not believe God has given them one jumped from 4% in 1995 to 21% in 2000.

They continued by saying:

One of the startling outcomes, however, was the number and range of gifts listed by born again adults that are not among the spiritual gifts listed in the Bible. Such "gifts" included a sense of humor, listening, patience, a good personality, friendliness, poetry, going to church, being likeable, drawing, survival, observation, and being a good person. In total, several dozen non-gifts were listed. Overall, the survey showed that among born again adults only 30% listed gifts found in the Bible.

Despite Biblical evidence to the contrary born again believers reported they did not have a spiritual gift. Time and again people listed personality attributes and erroneously labeled them spiritual gifts. They cited spiritual gifts that did not exist – spiritual gifts that were not spiritual gifts. These results suggest that many Christians do not know what spiritual gifts are much less which gifts they have been given.

We do not know what spiritual gifts are because we have not been taught. On those occasions when we have been taught the "concept" of spiritual gifts, we may have failed to grasp the personal nature of gifts. We may not have realized how intimate an act it is for God to give special gifts to us as tokens of our union with Him and as tools for the work we will do together.

Spiritual Gifts Have Been Isolated to the "Physical" Confines of the Church

Every time I hear someone speaking of a spiritual gift it is in the context of the church environment. I believe this is one of the most damaging aspects of the way we talk about gifts on those occasions when it is taught. Please don't misunderstand me, I love the church. I love my church and couldn't imagine a more exciting, relevant place to worship. But too often we take the tools God uses to execute his plan on earth – us and our gifts – and put them in a shed that is only opened on Sunday mornings and Wednesday nights.

When the Bible tells us that the gifts we have been given by the Holy Spirit are to be used for the church, it is not talking exclusively about my church, your church or any particular church. This is not a brick and mortar issue. It is a body of Christ issue. Of this Billy Graham said the following:

The word "Church" comes from the Greek word that

means "called together ones."... Every person who has
repented of his sin and received Jesus Christ as Savior
and Lord is a member of this body called the Church.
So the Church is more than a religious organization. It
is an organism with Christ as its living head. It is alive,
with the life of Christ made living in each member.[9]

The "call" from Jesus to do His will during our time on
earth comes in many different forms. Some are called to
pulpits, some to pin-stripes, some to nurse's outfits, and some
are simply called to be the "best street sweepers." The gifts we
have been given by God are not supposed to be shelved for
most of the week, then dusted off when we enter a church.

Gifts are for you and me to express and develop. They are
for today and tomorrow. They are for the physical church and
the larger body of Christ of which we are called to be an
integral part. Gifts are for tomorrow morning when I have to
face people in the corporate world, many of whom are
hurting, sad and living without hope. My gifts should be used
to provide hope and a lift that will get them through another
day. I pray that I will have an opportunity to teach them
about the reason for my hope. Through word, deed and
example, I will attempt to communicate the message of
abundance using the gifts He gave me.

I am heartbroken when I hear of gifts being spoken of
purely in the context of the church environment. There are
people who have different gift sets than I who are wonderful at
greeting people when they arrive in church. They solve
parking problems and escort people to their classrooms.
These are wonderful activities – necessary ones – and I do not
mean to minimize their impact. Using their gifts in the
physical church is exactly what they should be doing. But
these may not be activities that will cause someone to
celebrate the impact they have made on the world for Christ
as they lie on their deathbed. For that type of celebration we
must use our gifts for God's purpose
outside the physical church.

Outside the church environment there are people who look

like you and me, but they are hopeless and lost. They would give anything if someone with the spiritual gifts of hospitality and mercy would make them feel like they are accepted, loved and welcomed for once in their life.

Outside the church environment, where we have our social masks on, there are people who will go to Heaven when they die, but are living in hell while on earth. They live each day as the polar opposite of Romans 8:37. They are not "more than conquerors." They are beaten down, confused, and unclear about how to live in a victorious fashion in a world that is so hostile to dreams and abundant living. They would give anything if someone with the spiritual gifts of faith, mercy and encouragement would help them understand the true significance of their life. They want to believe their life has a purpose. They want to believe they are children of the King and "more than conquerors." Our gifts should help them believe.

Outside the church environment there are people who are breathing, but they are not alive. They have little or no hope. For them, there is no tomorrow. They have no dreams. There is no relationship with Jesus. Worst of all, one day these people will stop breathing and enter a period of everlasting torment because they are separated from God. As I heard someone once say, "There really is a Heaven and there really is a hell, and people really do go there." They desperately need us to use our spiritual gifts to impact their life in this life and beyond.

If someone has the gift of serving, let us not do them the disservice of suggesting that the use of that gift is purely a "church thing." That gift was given to them by the same Holy Spirit that breathed the very words of God into Peter, Paul, Stephen and the prophets of old. That same Spirit has given us these wonderful gifts and seeks nothing more or less than our all. God makes no partial demands on us. "You will seek me and find me when you seek me with all your heart" (Jer 29:13 NIV). He wants it all. He wants our full-time commitment. The last thing He wants us to do is to take that direct gift from Him and relegate it to a part time status.

Gifts are for your church, there is no question. But I propose that there is also no question that your gifts are for your life and for those who are influenced by your life. You cannot – and you will not – do what you are intended to do or be who you are supposed to be until you discover those gifts God has given you and commit to using them full time for His glory.

SPIRITUAL GIFTS

What follows is a list of the spiritual gifts with a brief description of each. This list and definitions are derived from *Gifts – The Joy of Serving God* by Ortberg, Pederson, and Polling; *Network: The Right People ... In the Right Places ... For the Right Reasons* by Bugbee, Cousins, and Hybels; and *Discover Your Spiritual Gifts* by C. Peter Wagner.

Some authors may include other gifts in their list and cite Biblical references for their additions. My intention is not to be all-inclusive, but to expose you to a list of spiritual gifts with simple definitions. From this list, we will be able to continue our discussion of gifts as the third element of abundance. I fully expect that as you explore your gifts you will need to use other resources. I have included a list of additional resources you can use to take you further into gifts than I am able to in this brief introduction.

As you read through this list consider the roles you play in Faith, Family, and Vocation and those areas where you are particularly strong or comfortable in each. This train of thought will help you identify your gifts and how they might have been employed in the various areas of your life. Also, know that for these definitions I have removed much of the language that points the spiritual gifts in the direction of God or the church. This was done intentionally to help you see yourself more clearly in the definitions. For example, a definition that indicates the gift is used to build the ministry might cause the sales professional to flip the page since she does not work for a church.

Please remember that spiritual gifts are the tools we use to glorify God. As such, in Faith, Family, and Vocation the actions we take using them should always point to and be pleasing in the sight of God. Also, know that the gifts you have don't change depending on the environment you are in. You may be able to see your gifts more clearly in a certain area of your life – that will likely be the case. But once discovered you must find a way to use those gifts in all areas of life.

Finally, as mentioned above I removed many references to the term "ministry" in defining the various spiritual gifts. Another reason I did so was because that term often lets too many of us off the hook. It allows too many people – like me – to think that gifts and ministries are for other people. Remember, all of us have a ministry and full time Kingdom work if we are living as we should. That ministry may involve preaching and teaching or the more subtle forms of influence you use in the workplace. So please consider expanding the term ministry to include what God is doing or wants to do through your life, your church, your business, or your family. In Faith, Family, and Vocation we are to use the gifts God gave us for those various ministries. Here is the list of gifts with definitions for each:

> **Administration:** Ability to organize people, tasks, or events in order to achieve the goals of an organization or ministry. Able to develop strategies, increase efficiency, and thrives on bringing order out of chaos.
>
> **Apostleship:** Ability to start new churches, ministries, or programs and oversee their development.
>
> **Craftsmanship:** Ability to design or construct items or effectively work with tools. May work with a variety of materials to include wood, cloth, metal, and glass.
>
> **Creative Communications:** Ability to communicate through the use of art. May be gifted in art, music, drama, dance, or writing.
>
> **Discernment:** Ability to distinguish between truth and error, various motives, or the presence of evil. Can see right or wrong clearly as well as inconsistencies in teaching or actions.
>
> **Encouragement:** Ability to strengthen, comfort, or urge to action those who are discouraged or wavering in

their faith. Looks to uplift others and provide hope for the future.

Evangelism: Ability to effectively communicate the gospel in a compelling way. This is often related to a pastoral role. But, it may also be seen in those individuals who are very effective in getting a conversation to the point where they can "evangelize" or communicate the truth of God.

Faith: Ability to act on God's promises with confidence and unwavering belief. May be those people who refuse to give up; they maintain their confidence and belief when others are falling away. By example alone are able to strengthen and give confidence to others.

Giving: Ability to contribute money and resources to the work of the Lord with cheerfulness and liberality. May be gifted with the ability to make large sums of money and the desire to give back to the community, the church, and God in recognition of those blessings.

Healing: Ability to be human intermediaries through whom it pleases God to cure illness or restore health apart from the use of natural means.

Hospitality: Ability to joyfully create an environment that welcomes others and puts them at ease. These are people who go out of their way to ensure others are comfortable.

Intercession: Ability to consistently and passionately pray on behalf of others. These are the people who say "I'll pray for you" and actually do it consistently.

Interpretation: Ability to make known the message of one who speaks in tongues.

Knowledge: Ability to bring truth to the body of Christ through deep Biblical insight and understanding.

Leadership: Ability to cast vision, motivate, and direct people to collectively accomplish the purpose of a group or organization. Able to help people see where they need to go in order to move toward a better tomorrow.

Mercy: Ability to cheerfully and practically help those who are suffering or are in need. Comes alongside those who are in need; willing to help the downtrodden; has a real heart for those who need helping hand.

Miracles: Ability to serve as human intermediaries through whom it pleases God to perform powerful acts that are perceived by observers to have altered the ordinary course of nature.

Prophecy: Ability to reveal truth and proclaim it in a timely and relevant manner for understanding, correction, repentance or edification.

Serving: Ability to accomplish practical and necessary tasks to support needs or free-up others to use their gifts. Able to work behind the scenes and feel the reward that comes from doing the little things it takes to make a church or organization function.

Shepherding: Ability to nurture and guide people in proper directions. People with this gift may naturally gravitate toward a mentor role where they can help another along a journey.

Teaching: Ability to understand, clearly explain, and apply material and concepts in a manner that will help others. People with this gift may feel best when teaching something to someone – the process of teaching is very rewarding to them.

Tongues: Ability to speak, worship, or pray in a language unknown to the speaker.

Wisdom: Ability to apply spiritual truth effectively to meet a need in a specific situation. Able to "see the big picture" clearly and step back from the chaos of life in order to apply God's truth to situations.

FINDING YOUR GIFTS

"When God gifted you, he took into account your uniqueness – your background, temperament, likes, passions. As you live consistently with your unique pattern of giftedness, you will make the specific contribution God designed you to make."[10] It is important that we find and employ our gifts because they are intricately tied to the "specific contribution God designed you to make."

Discovering your spiritual gifts is among the most important things that you must do as a Christ follower. It is a requirement for living the abundant life. We are all given these gifts and it is up to us to learn what they are, then employ them to their fullest and best use. But how do we do it? If spiritual gifts are those endowments granted to me by God, how do I find what my gifts are?

A detailed description of the exact journey you should take to find your spiritual gifts is beyond both the scope of this book and my level of expertise. The first step though is entering into a relationship with Jesus, and in so doing, joining with the Holy Spirit for the journey. This joining is an intimate act that each of us must do individually. When this occurs Jesus tells us that the Holy Spirit "will teach you all things and will remind you of everything I have said to you" (Jn 14:26 NIV). He also instructs us that the Spirit will "guide you into all truth" (Jn 16:13 NIV) and "bring glory to me (Jesus) by taking from what is mine and making it known to you" (Jn 16:14 NIV).

Through your relationship with Jesus and the truth you receive, you can begin to understand those gifts you have been given and the manner in which you are to use them. The journey toward discovering your spiritual gifts will be a personal one. That being said, there are some approaches to this discovery that I will recommend as you begin the journey toward finding your spiritual gifts.

Read – Read on the topic of spiritual gifts and the Holy Spirit. That simple act will enable you to become more knowledgeable of spiritual gifts and the work of the Holy Spirit. As a starting point I would recommend the following:

The Holy Spirit – Activating God's Power in Your Life
    by Billy Graham
Gifts – The Joy of Serving God by Ortberg, Pederson,
    and Polling

Network: The Right People … In the Right Places … For the Right Reasons by Bugbee, Cousins, and Hybels.

Study – The above references will help illuminate the topic of spiritual gifts and provide a level of detail not contained in this book. However, the ultimate study guide on spiritual gifts is the Bible. The following verses contain direct or indirect references to spiritual gifts and would be the ultimate written Word on the topic of spiritual gifts:

Romans 12:4-8
1 Corinthians 12:1-27
Ephesians 4:4-8
1 Peter 4:9-11

Reflect – Take a look at your life to this point and identify those propensities that might indicate spiritual gifts at work. Are you the one who winds up leading everything you are involved in, even when you don't necessarily want to? Do you end up taking care of sick family members or friends and have the ability to be with someone who is downtrodden for hours, even days, at a time? Instead of just saying that you will pray for someone, do you actually maintain a consistent prayer routine with that person on your list? Do you find yourself praying for virtually everything and everyone with a strong faith that you are being heard and that your prayer makes a difference?

You might realize that you are always doing certain things when you truly feel fulfilled at work. It may involve encouraging those around you, lifting their spirits and giving them hope. It may entail putting processes in place and bringing order out of chaos. Those feelings of fulfillment may always be related to times when you are teaching someone to do something. These may be indications of spiritual gifts or propensities for those gifts that are at work in your life.

Pray – Pray that the Holy Spirit will make clear to you what your spiritual gifts are. Reading, studying, reflecting, these are all ways in which you can build your knowledge level in order to facilitate the discovery and learning process. Ultimately the

Helper – the Holy Spirit – will guide you through the process of learning and understanding your spiritual gifts. Prayer is the manner in which you communicate with God and by which you approach the throne of grace with your requests. Through prayer you can ask God to illuminate the path along the journey toward discovering your spiritual gifts and to help you use those gifts for His purposes.

Discuss – Seek a trusted advisor or mentor who you can talk with about your spiritual gifts. This advisor will need to be someone who is spiritually mature and knowledgeable of spiritual gifts. As you study, reflect, and pray about your spiritual gifts this advisor could be someone that could help guide you through the process of discovery. Sometimes this person can help you see strengths or characteristics you might not be fully aware of. Conversely, they might help you with a reality check if you are leaning toward spiritual gifts that you desire but might not have. As with most things, perception and reality might not always be the same thing – the advisor can help with this process.

Inventory – Do a spiritual gifts inventory. The final recommendation on finding your spiritual gifts is to use the formal tools available to do just that. There are a number of spiritual gifts inventories that are very helpful in identifying what your spiritual gifts might be. One is included in *Network: The Right People ... In the Right Places ... For the Right Reasons* by Bugbee, Cousins, and Hybels. I recommend using an inventory to confirm your suspicions at the end of the process rather than at the beginning. It is important to use knowledge, reflection, communications with God, and communications with spiritually mature advisors as the primary channels through which we discover our spiritual gifts.

An inventory can be used at the end to clarify or verify your gift set. At the beginning, though, you might fall into the trap of replacing reflection, prayer, study, and dialogue with the results of a 20-minute survey. It would be easy to take the top three gifts in our survey and say those are our spiritual gifts. It would be easy to take the shortcut. Unfortunately there are few shortcuts that really shorten the journey. Going the extra mile to consider your gifts, study about them, and pray about them beforehand will take you further along the path to discovery than any "quick fix" approach to answering the question of your spiritual gifts.

PASSION, BURDEN, VISION, AND GIFTS

There is a passion that resonates with our soul. This passion keeps us in an elevated state as we seek to satisfy the hungers that result from such passion. The burden we bear represents our cross and keeps the passion properly contained and centered on our life in Jesus. Our God-ordained vision keeps us focused on bringing about a tomorrow that is consistent with why God put us on the face of the earth. Our gifts help us determine what the journey will look like and what our specific contribution will be.

My passion is "leadership; connecting with and lifting people." My burden is "the lack of victory, joy, and significance in the life of God's children." My vision is "children of the King living out their John 10:10 inheritance." To say that I want desperately for all people to understand that the abundant life is waiting for them would be an understatement. I want to scream it from the mountaintop. But without an understanding of my gift set, I am not able to know what God wants me to do with my passion, burden and vision.

My gifts are leadership, encouragement and teaching. I like to think of these gifts as giant clues as to whether I am supposed to be involved in something or not. We all have to be involved in activities that are outside our realm of giftedness. But as we mature spiritually we should be consciously trying to spend more time in our area of giftedness. Like a sweet spot on a baseball bat or tennis racket – an area where the hit just feels so natural – activities that employ our spiritual gifts feel so right and tend to bring out the best that we have to offer. They tap into a special reservoir of talent placed in us by God.

If I do not know where that sweet spot is (the work or activity I can do that fits my God-given gifts), I might try to fulfill my vision in ways that are outside my realm of giftedness. I might have a vision of helping people live abundant lives and for uplifting those encountering difficulties. Because of this vision, I could spend days by a hospital bedside and speak of abundance during those periods when the person I am sitting with is coherent enough to have a discussion. During the times the patient is not lucid I could be by his side offering comfort by my presence. Such may be the nature of someone with the gift of mercy.

Unfortunately, I am not blessed with that gift. The problem is that I would surely make the person more ill by my very presence. Because of my gift set I would last about 15 minutes before I started trying to encourage the sickness out of his body, asking him to take a few steps toward recovery in the full expectation that he would be running sprints toward good health in no time. It is important to know where my gifts align me for usefulness and where I am a natural "square peg in a round hole."

The need to understand gifts and how they relate to your vision applies to all the different areas of your life – Faith, Family, and Vocation. You need to know what you can "bring to the table" and what you cannot. For example, your gifts may serve as a clue that you are probably not very good at showing mercy. If your spouse is going through a circumstance where you need to exhibit merciful characteristics you can:

(A) Explain that what your spouse needs is outside your area of giftedness.
(B) Call someone else to administer the gift to your spouse.
(C) Dutifully and compassionately step outside your area of giftedness and show as much mercy and caring that you can muster.

Knowing your gifts can help you focus on doing those things you are wired by God to do. But, as illustrated in the multiple choice scenario above, knowing your gifts can also help you gain awareness of those areas in which you are not strong.

Since you do not have a choice but to function in some of those areas you must be very disciplined in reacting promptly to things that fall outside your area of giftedness. By the way, if you did not pick answer "C" in the above example please put this book down immediately and read some books on marriage!

Knowing your gift set will help you determine how to carry out the vision that you have for tomorrow. There are so many people working in jobs that simply do not use the gifts that God gave them. While this may be required for periods of time – there are bills to be paid – the long term impact of working outside of your giftedness can be tragic.

Can you picture someone in your organization who is very good at what they do, perhaps highly compensated for it, but you can tell they do not enjoy it? Can you envision someone in your mind who is incredibly talented, but wanders from job to job because nothing provides long term satisfaction? Can you think of someone whose disposition suggests maturity when in actuality they just stopped asking as much from life as they used to and settled for mediocrity? Can you see them where you work? Can you see them in your church? Can you see them in your mirror?

When we allow ourselves to fall into a pattern of spending 8-10 hours per day performing tasks that do not use the gifts God gave us, we essentially barricade ourselves from working hand-in-hand with the Holy Spirit. We cannot allow our gifts to go unused if we want to live the abundant, victorious, joy-filled life that Jesus came that we might have.

Because of that I had to make a decision some time ago about my own career. I can honestly say it's easy for me to say "yes" to new challenges. I love change and new opportunities. However, I committed that all changes have to pass the "gift" test. That means any new opportunities would have to allow me to spend a significant portion of time working in my area of giftedness.

I, like you, have worked for periods of time outside my giftedness. Sometimes that is necessary for several reasons. First, the destination of our journey is not always direct. It often requires that we have experiences to help us clarify exactly where it is that we are supposed to go. There's nothing like traveling down the wrong road to convince you to get back on the right one. Working outside your realm of giftedness can feel like that wrong road, but can bring clarity into your life.

Second, sometimes working outside our realm of giftedness is a price we must pay in order to reach the level that allows us to maximize the use of our gifts. There have been extremely gifted pastors who had to "endure" working with children's ministries that were outside their gift set. There are incredible leaders who have to suffer through administratively intense positions in order to put themselves in a position to maximize the use of their leadership gift. There is a price to be paid for these experiences and it may just be a part of God's intended journey for our lives.

The problem is that we often start walking into quicksand when we develop a pattern of working outside our giftedness. We justify it. We call it temporary. We call it necessary. We forget that we are given these gifts by God and that He has not called us for part time service.

This I know. The higher up the ladder you go, be it on a corporate organization chart or a church hierarchy, the harder it is to work outside your realm of giftedness and make it "back to the other side." If you are earning $150,000 per year in an area outside of your giftedness, it is extraordinarily difficult to walk away for the sake of your God-given gift. Please don't misunderstand me. I am not suggesting that we should be monks living in poverty or that if we are making a great income, we are doing something wrong. I do not believe that or intend to apply that rationale to my own life!

What I will state emphatically is that our income is not the best litmus test for how we are doing in carrying out the will of God in our lives. A six-figure salary does not necessarily mean we are tapping into the best part of ourselves – the part God gave to each of us individually. If we can earn all of that on our own merits, what could we do if we actually let God work through us? What would happen if we used the spiritual gifts God gave us so His generosity could flow through us? That generosity could flow in the form of material wealth or it might not. But if it is flowing from God, there is no doubt that we will have tapped into a source of riches unequaled by any salary or incentive structure.

What does this mean in "the real world?" To me it means there are jobs that would appear to be a promotion that I would not accept simply because they would cause me to depart radically from my realm of giftedness. Could I do them? Yes! Would I be fulfilled? Would I feel positively challenged? Would I live the abundant life? Certainly not. Abundance cannot survive when what we are doing is separated from our area of giftedness.

In our Faith walk it is no different. It is absolutely imperative that we figure out what tools we have been given to do the work God puts before us. We have all been called to "Go into all the world and preach the Good News to everyone, everywhere (Mk 16:15 NLT)." This means that we must spread the message we have received in ways that will build the Kingdom. But just like a construction project, Kingdom work needs workers with a variety of skills to complete the work. Our part, no matter how seemingly small or large, is necessary. The specific, personal combination of gifts given by the Master to each of us makes us the master craftsmen for some element of Kingdom work. Let us use our gifts accordingly.

GIFTS AND ABUNDANCE

The emptiness that we so often feel in our lives may be traced back to our distance from God. No matter what measure of success we use there will always be a void if we do not have the personal relationship with Him that He intended. We know that we need Him and sometimes we truly want Him with all of our heart. But we are often confused about how to firmly establish and maintain a personal relationship with Jesus.

There are so many struggles inherent in maintaining this personal relationship and just as many best practices for keeping your relationship strong. I propose that one of the pathways to this relationship and to God is through your spiritual gifts. We have each been given at least one spiritual gift that is to be used to glorify God. These gifts represent an interaction and exchange between man and the Holy Spirit. This conveying of gifts from the Holy Spirit makes spiritual gifts particularly personal. Gifts are the tools given to us by the God who created the universe so that we might act as His fellow workers on a daily basis.

Using our spiritual gifts means that we know what the fingerprints of God look like in our life. He has reached down into a human being and placed something upon us and upon our children, that reflects His plan for our life. Isn't that an incredibly powerful and humbling thought?

The God of the universe has given us special combinations of abilities that no one else has. There are things that He wants us to do with those special abilities that are different from the responsibilities of everyone else in the universe. These gifts are ours and ours alone from God.

Spiritual gifts help make God personal. They serve as a reminder that this huge God that we serve takes the time to give to each of us individually. He has a plan for us, has given us the tools to carry out that plan, and has told us that all of His plans have the same thing in common: "For I know the plans I have for you ... They are plans for good and not for disaster, to give you a future and a hope" (Jer 29:11 NLT).

Spiritual gifts have for too long been left on the sideline. We wonder why we don't feel fulfilled at our work and in our church. We wonder why we don't get as much satisfaction as we used to. Even when we tap into our passion and vision we sometimes veer off course and are perplexed at how things could go so wrong when our vision looked so right.

To live the abundant life – where our cup overflows with joy and we are walking and working in concert with God's designs for our lives – we must know what tools He has given us for the work to be done. Our gifts cannot be left unused if we are to live abundantly. To live the abundant life, we must live consistent with God's designs for our lives. And God's designs always include using what He has given us and glorifying Him in all that we do.

Spiritual gifts are the third element of abundance. With

passion we discussed what God caused us to care deeply about. Burden is the cross that we bear that keeps our passion related and pointed to God. Vision is the God-ordained plan for our lives, and takes into account the fact that we are destined to do specific work for the Kingdom by virtue of being children of the King. Spiritual gifts are those abilities that we are hard-wired with by God in order to do the work that He has put us here to do.

He gave us the heart to do something (passion); He gave us an image of what we are to do (vision); and He gave us the tools or implements of our trade in order to carry out the plan (gifts). That is the role of spiritual gifts in the journey toward abundance. Gifts are given for Kingdom work. We are created for Kingdom work. When we live abundantly everything we do is Kingdom work.

PERSONAL REFLECTIONS

What are your gifts?

How might you use your gifts in your Vocation?

Living the Abundant Life

How might you use your gifts with your Family?

How might you use your gifts in you Faith?

Bryan Collier, pastor of The Orchard in Tupelo, Mississippi, applies a challenging question to many decisions he makes: Who will be glorified, God or me? Using Bryan's question as a guide, answer each of the following questions:

Have you been using your gifts to glorify God or yourself?

How can you use your gifts so that God is glorified and that you take your place as an integral part of the Kingdom drama that is unfolding?

6

INTERSECTION

Passion is the first element of abundance. It is what God caused you to care deeply about. Burden is the cross you bear that keeps your Passion pointed to God. Burden must always be Passion's anchor if you are to live the abundant life.

Vision is the second element of abundance. It is the God-ordained plan for where you are to go in life. Vision takes into account the fact that we are all destined to do specific work for the Kingdom by virtue of our being children of the King.

Spiritual Gifts are the third element of abundance. Knowing your spiritual gifts means knowing what tools God gave you to carry out the work that He has designed you for. Gifts are those abilities that you are hard-wired with by God in order to do the work that He has put you here to do.

The elements of abundance constantly point us to God as the source of life and the only True Satisfier of our needs and desires. Gaining clarity about our Passion, Burden, Vision, and Gifts helps us move closer to God and realize our true purpose for being. Can you imagine the intensity, the sense of purpose emanating from the person who is living in concert with God's designs – every day?

To live the abundant life that Jesus came to give us, we must come to understand our Passion, our Burden, our Vision, and our Gifts. But, while knowing the components of an abundant life is an essential part of the journey, that knowledge alone will not get you to the final destination. In other words, being able to name your Passion, reflect on your Burden, clearly see your

Vision, and know your Gifts are critical, but they are not enough to lay claim to the abundant life. To live the abundant life, you must also have the fourth element of abundance – Intersection. Before I define the Intersection, let me share a history lesson with you.

THE CIVIL WAR – GENERAL GEORGE B. MCCLELLAN

General George B. McClellan was hailed as the savior of the North when the Civil War erupted. This polished officer had served with General Winfield Scott in Mexico, alongside Robert E. Lee, and was widely regarded as a very capable Commander when he was named to head the Northern forces. Indeed, General McClellan, ("young Napoleon" as he was hailed by some) immediately started whipping the rag-tag forces of the Union army into shape. He instilled discipline into the ranks while marching these newly reformed troops in front of the throngs of observers in Washington, DC. General McClellan built discipline into the soldiers, made them feel proud of their accomplishments, and generated feelings of trust and confidence in the civilian population with the parading of the troops. A brilliant move!

Why then was General McClellan, a bright and shining star from his days at West Point and the reigning Commandant in the Union Army, ultimately removed from his position? Why was he consistently outclassed in battle by military commanders considered by himself and others as inferiors? Why had he evoked the ire of President Abraham Lincoln, who voiced his frustration when he commented: "If General McClellan isn't going to use his army, I'd like to borrow it for a time."

I believe one explanation for these dramatic failures on the part of such a capable commander is that General McClellan lived his life and underwrote his leadership with a mentality that rendered him incapable of winning the war. He was brilliant at organizing his command. He was incredible at training the troops to fight. He mastered the art of planning for

Living the Abundant Life

logistical support. He even excelled at gaining and maintaining political support for his cause. At what, then, did he fail?

General McClellan failed to fully understand that war required loss. He failed to realize that war and uncertainty go hand in hand. He failed to comprehend that war and courage are inseparable and that war is chaotic, even when the odds are stacked in your favor. He was never comfortable stepping off into that chaos. Unfortunately for him, the genteel, statesman-like character on the other side of the conflict, Robert E. Lee, was masterful at managing chaos and focused on destroying the enemy, or "those people," as he called the opposing forces. The results were not positive for General McClellan.

General McClellan spent too much time at an "ego altitude," which kept him from mustering up the courage or resolve to consistently bring his influence to bear at ground level. It was there that his army would have actually been employed to engage the enemy. It was there that his carefully crafted creation could have been used for its intended purpose – winning the war. Because of this failure to act, McClellan soon became irrelevant and was fired, despite his administrative brilliance.

CORPORATE AMERICA

In many ways, the corporate executive or church leader of today runs the risk of falling into the same trap that General McClellan did during the Civil War. His problem was, in essence, an altitude problem.

The executive who spends his time at 20,000 feet in altitude gains a macro view of his company. Some may feel that this view provides the best indication of what is truly going on in the company. Able to distance himself from the noise of the minutia, this executive can see more clearly where the organization is going and what kind of overriding vision he needs to apply in order to facilitate the movement in the proper direction.

Unfortunately this is not what usually happens when executives spend their time at 20,000 feet. When they spend too much time in "rarified air," they usually suffer from what I call the corporate equivalent of "nitrogen narcosis." This condition, a result of breathing compressed air at certain depths while scuba diving, can result in an altered mental state similar to alcohol intoxication. It can cause the person suffering from it to exhibit characteristics that range from being goofy, acting irrationally, feeling like they can fly, having a sense of indestructibility, and possibly even exhibiting a king complex. Does that describe any executives you know?

My point is that many executives fall into the trap of living at such an altitude that they lose connection with what is going on in the real world. For example, Chainsaw Al Dunlap became a common name in business circles years ago because of his "slash and burn" tactics in companies he was hired to turn around. For a time it appeared that his methods were successful. He even wrote a book lauding his "Mean Business" methods. Eventually those methods were proven to be faulty and he was shown to be someone who operated at an altitude so high that he forgot those pawns in his grand schemes were actually human beings. The cost to the people and the cost to those companies he destroyed were great indeed. It revealed the potential dangers from someone who does not take into account the ripple effects of his "higher level" decisions.

Max Depree said "the first responsibility of a leader is to define reality."[1] The examples we have looked at were of people who failed to accurately define reality as the rest of the world saw it. They paid a price for this failure. They always do, and so do we!

GETTING ON THE BALCONY

In contrast to the examples above, consider the advice Ronald Heifetz and Marty Linsky give to leaders.[2] They suggest that many times we lead from the perspective of one who is on the dance floor. We are out there with our partner whirling around to the sound of the music. As we look around, we might observe how crowded the dance floor is and how much everyone seems to enjoy the band. As the band plays the final song, we might logically conclude that everyone will go home eager to return to such a wonderful environment.

In fact, what we do not understand is that our limited perspective biased our interpretation of the night. Heifetz and Linsky point out that if we were really observant, we would have noticed there were very few people dancing. Those who were, including us, were congregated in one small corner of the dance floor. Most of the crowd did not enjoy the band and expressed their opinion by remaining off the dance floor or leaving early.

They would say we need to occasionally get off the dance floor and move up to the balcony in order to gain the proper perspective. On the balcony we could see the large dance floor only partially occupied. We could see the reactions of those who did not dance. We could watch as they went home early.

The suggestion would be that we need to move up to 20,000 feet – on the balcony – in order to see and understand these things. But isn't that the problem we just looked at? Isn't that exactly what General McClellan and the executive did? Didn't that cause them to fail miserably?

Yes, and no. They followed part of the prescription that Heifetz and Linsky provide – they got on the balcony. What they failed to do is to get off the balcony and get back on the dance floor. They failed to realize that our time on the balcony and the dance floor represents a constant flow back and forth, not unlike the ebb and flow of the tide. There is a routine movement between high and low tide, and there should be a routine movement between balcony perspectives and dance floor action. A failure to build both into our perspective in leadership – and in life – will result in a failure to accurately define reality.

I have admitted throughout this book that I am obsessed with the topic of leadership, but have tried to refrain from lacing the text with leadership stories, lessons, and examples. Even as I wrote the above narrative, I wondered if I was crossing the line by mixing leadership with abundant living. I don't believe I have.

McClellan's leadership failure and Chainsaw Dunlap's management style bear striking similarities despite the years that separated their shortcomings. The need to move back and forth from the dance floor to the balcony is timeless in its application. It is also directly related to the Intersection as the fourth element of abundance.

PERSONAL REFLECTIONS

In what ways or areas of your life (Faith, Family, Vocation) might you be too close to the action, the fray on the dance floor, to see the bigger picture?

In what ways or areas of your life (Faith, Family, Vocation) might you be too withdrawn, too isolated, too insulated – spending too much time on the balcony – to really be engaged in a manner that can positively impact the world you are supposed to be living in?

Passion, Burden, Vision, and Gifts: These are the thoughts and guiding principles of one who is trying to live life on a different level. The ability to reflect consistently on these matters, to bring clarity in these areas, will take you a long way down the path toward abundance. Unfortunately, these lofty ideals could become balcony ideas. These can be the thoughts of someone who is separated – anesthetized – from the realities of living in the real world.

These can also be the thoughts of someone whose flirtations with abundance are usually temporal in nature. The person reflecting on these things all day long will one day have to face the fact that the world as he or she envisions it and the one that actually exists are two different places. Oswald Chambers pointed out that we often live for those times on the mount of transfiguration – when we are truly who we desire to be and are in perfect union with God.[3] We wish that we could spend all of our lives in that moment of perfect union and wholeness.

Unfortunately, those times may be few and far between. Chambers points out quite accurately that while we love the time on the mount of transfiguration, we live in the valley. It is in the valley – with all of its difficulties, monotony, and minutiae, that we spend the vast majority of our life.

Thus far I have sought to convince you that Passion, Vision, and Gifts are the first three elements of abundance. Now, I am suggesting that these things can lead to temporary frills, to disillusionment, and to a separation from a position of abundance and relevance in the world. To live an abundant life, where you are living as you should and having the proper impact, you might need to consider a piece of wisdom I will borrow from the Chinese.

Chinese lore tends to idealize the recluse. This may be the man who ascends the mountains above the Yangtze River for a life of contemplation and quietude. He and his chosen lifestyle are often celebrated in Chinese culture. However, I once read that the great recluse is not the mountain recluse. Instead the

"Great Recluse is the city recluse."[4] The city recluse is the one who lives amidst the hustle and bustle of every day life yet maintains his peace and balance. He does not need to take a station at the top of a mountain where he can reflect all day long, but have an impact on no one. The city recluse is able to live in those lofty places, even if only in his mind, yet come down enough to actually have an impact on the world. That is the perfect recluse.

To live the abundant life, you must maintain your focus on the lofty ideals, you must be on the balcony, you must have a reclusive and reflective outlook on life that enables you to gain clarity and restore peace routinely. But you must also regularly exercise the option of returning to the dance floor, living amidst the noise, confusion, and rush of life as the city recluse. This will ensure that your outlook is both laced with reality and has the opportunity to be used for good purposes where it is most needed – in the real world.

That work, that Passion, that Burden, that God-ordained Vision cannot be satisfied through mental exercises, or with the mere plans of a dreamer. For these things to be satisfied and for abundance to be yours, you must live the life. You must bring these elements together – to a point – and bring them there regularly. In so doing you will continuously be reminded of why you are here, and you will also receive the incredible, unparalleled affirmation that comes from knowing you are doing exactly what God wants you to do. That point is the Intersection.

Do you have enough "reclusive tendencies" in your schedule to allow you to recharge your batteries, reconnect with your priorities, strengthen the bond with your family, and grow in relationship with Jesus? If no, how can you build these into your calendar?

How can you prioritize those reclusive moments, yet stay fully engaged in life, moving back and forth from the balcony to the dance floor?

THE INTERSECTION — WHAT EXACTLY IS IT?

Simply stated, the Intersection is that point where Passion, Vision, and Gifts come together in the life of a child of God. The Intersection is where who you are and what you are doing merge, thereby putting you squarely on the path of abundance. You are doing what you are and are able to say, "What I do is me. For this I came." That is the Intersection.

Let me try and illustrate both the power and the need for a well-defined Intersection. Passion is the first element of abundance and creates quite a stir within us. When we start tapping into a reservoir of Passion, we discover sources of energy never before discovered or dormant for a long period of time. Indeed, Passion energizes our steps and sends us off in the direction it desires we travel.

Did you notice that subtlety? Passion sends us off in the direction that IT would have us travel. There is an element of power and control to Passion's call and direction that beckons us constantly to follow. Passion's impact is such in our life that it literally propels us in the direction of that Passion. In physics you might say that Passion causes a vector of energy to emanate from us in the direction of that Passion.

In each of the illustrations below, the circles represent what occurs when the elements of abundance are introduced into our life. The lines represent the vectors of energy that are created by the elements of abundance. Passion, then, might look something like this:

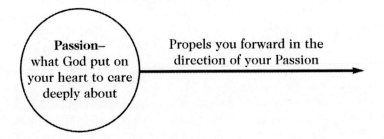

Passion strikes you and sends a vector out into the world, providing direction and momentum to move forward. It energizes your life. At the same time, this newfound clarity about your Vision sends forth its own vector and likewise provides direction and momentum. You begin to understand what you want to accomplish in your Faith, Family, and Vocation as well as an overall Vision for your life. Vision then might look like this:

Living the Abundant Life

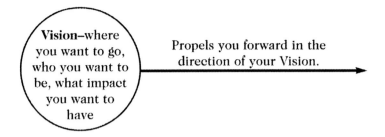

The problem is that too often Passion and Vision are completely separate or competing elements. We may feel Passion about some things in our life and have a Vision, but the elements never combine in a way that allows us to live as one person, whether at work or at home. We might drive 90 miles an hour in the pursuit of excellence at work (a Vision) and 90 miles an hour in the pursuit of something else at home (a Passion).

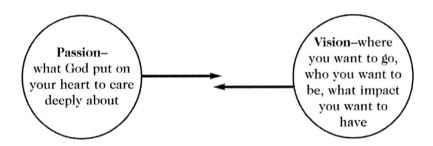

But we never really get anywhere because home and work seem to be elements that are competing for our time instead of being interrelated. Passion and Vision are both in place, but because there is no synergy between the two, no common direction or common goal, there is no real progress. When the elements of abundance compete rather than compliment each other, there will never be progress.

Take, for example, a woman who has a heart for God. She desires nothing more than to live out His will for her life. She takes solace in the time she spends at church and with her small study group. It is there that she feels she is doing something that really has lasting impact. Because of this she takes on every commitment that comes her way as it relates to her church activities. She does so because they represent an outgrowth of her Passion.

At work she sprints all day, every day, trying to increase the sales proficiency of her team. She has a Vision for her team being the best in her company. She also knows that sales and energy go hand-in-hand and has to deliver her best every time she walks in the door. She enjoys what she does, but doesn't quite know what to do with the competition for energy that sometimes occurs between her work and her Passion.

Her Passion seems noble and her Vision reasonable. There is nothing wrong with either except for the fact that while both consume her, they also pull her in opposite directions. To her, they represent mutually exclusive parts of her life. She has to be one person, then another, but does not know how to integrate them. She wears several favorite masks.

Her struggle is much like ours. We travel 90 miles an hour all day, every day and end up getting a "net zero" in terms of miles traveled and distance gained toward achieving our life goal. We sprint until we can barely breathe and all we really have to show for it is the fact that we are absolutely worn out. We end up losing our value to others and to the world with every passing moment of panicked, hurried living.

We don't wear ourselves out because we're necessarily doing the wrong things. Pastors are great examples of people who burn themselves out routinely, though they appear to be doing all the right things. One problem is they don't take care of the elements of abundance. Their Passion and Vision may be competing, not complimentary. They may find themselves serving certain needs all day long, when that is not their Passion or their Vision. Are those things necessary? Yes, perhaps they are. But when Passion and Vision work against each other, you will have no abundance, you will have no peace, you will have no rest. You will travel 90 mph all day, every day – and get nowhere. That will wear you out.

Add the third element of abundance and you start getting a clearer picture of both the abundant life and the reason many

Living the Abundant Life

falter. Knowing your Gifts entails knowing the tools God has given you as His fellow worker. It is an awesome thought to know that the Creator of the universe gave something specific to you so that you might build a certain portion of His Kingdom. That is incredible.

But in the quest for abundance, Gifts may seem difficult to employ on a day-by-day basis. The reason is similar to what we encountered when we looked at the above example. First, you may not know what your Gifts are. In that case the result is simple. Energy does not emerge, so no vector will be sent into the world.

Alternatively, you may discover your Gift and grow confident in what God has given you. In that case, a vector of energy is generated from your life as your Gifts propel you forward. Using the same illustrations as before it might look like this:

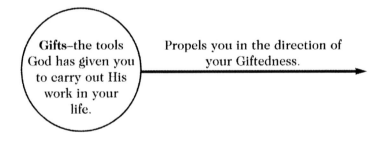

You may, however, find yourself employing your Gifts on a part-time basis. You may have discovered your Gifts in a church and have never used them outside of that setting. In fact, you may not have known there was any relevance to any setting other than the church. Therefore, your Gifts did not find their way into the main stream of your life. This would be one way that the energy generated by your Gifts could be stunted or even stopped.

Hopefully, at this point, you buy in to the need to make Gifts a full-time focus. God gave them to you individually, and the Bible is so clear on your need to know and use your Gifts. Believing in Gifts is not difficult to do when the facts are presented.

The following scenarios represent problems that could result if we are not mindful of the manner in which Gifts are employed and how they tie into Passion, Vision, and abundance.

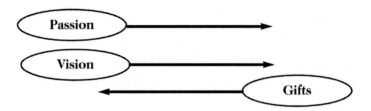

In this example, Passion and Vision are moving in the same direction. They seem to be in harmony. But Gifts – though they have been discovered and are creating direction, focus, and energy -- are not in harmony with the other elements of abundance.

Doesn't that sound esoteric? Let's try to shed some light on this example. A certain man's Passion is helping others become fully committed followers of Jesus. His Vision is for his company and his employees to reflect the life of Jesus. Because of this Passion and Vision, he actively witnesses to everyone within earshot and is constantly preaching the name of Jesus to those in his company. The problem? His gifts are administration and mercy. He is a capable business owner. He loves Jesus. But he is also as boring as a rock and takes an hour to explain a one minute principle.

He doesn't have the ability to preach these people into his Vision. He doesn't realize he is trying to use Gifts he does not have to fulfill his Passion and Vision. Meanwhile his God-given spiritual Gifts are not being used for his God-ordained Vision and God-inspired Passion. The elements of abundance are there, but are not working together. In this scenario there will be no abundance. It is not enough to know your Passion, your Vision, and your Gifts. There has to be a complimentary relationship among these elements to live the abundant life.

Here is one more scenario:

Living the Abundant Life

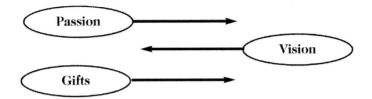

In this case the Passion and Gifts are moving in the same direction. Suppose the Passion is for growing and encouraging people, and the Gifts are encouragement and teaching. The Vision is for an organization to double in size every four years for the next 20 years. Anyone who has ever been in such an organization will recognize the tone of that Vision. Growth, growth, growth. When you commit to growth, you are making a statement about where your values are and what you are going to do with barriers – you are going to plow right through them.

First, there is nothing wrong with growth. I'm not criticizing that strategy. What I am calling into question is the consistency between the stated Passion (growing and encouraging people), the Gifts (encouragement and teaching), and the Vision (double the organization every four years for the next 20 years).

Passion and Gifts are in alignment and have consistency in the focus on people – growing, encouraging, and teaching them. The stated Vision does not capture this aspect at all. It simply speaks of the growth of the organization. Now let's be honest. If you spend your time growing, encouraging, and teaching people, will your organization grow? I believe it will. I hope it will! But the point here is that the stated Vision does not intersect with the Passion and Gifts. It would be too easy to forget about the Passion and Gifts, and only focus on the Vision.

When the Vision is not coming true, when the growth is not quite as expected, what might this person do? Would he or she do whatever it takes to grow? Would he or she still have the focus on building those in the organization as the organization grew? Would the individuals in the organization get the same priority as the organization itself? (What is the organization anyway but its people?) When stressors are applied, there could be points of separation between the Passion, Vision, and Gifts that could cause discord. In so doing, we neutralize the elements of abundance and their subsequent impact on our journey to abundance.

INTERSECTION — SO WHAT DO WE DO THEN?

What we need to do is employ the Intersection as the final element of abundance. It is my belief that the Intersection is perhaps the most important element of abundance. Let's look at another illustration and discuss the importance of the Intersection.

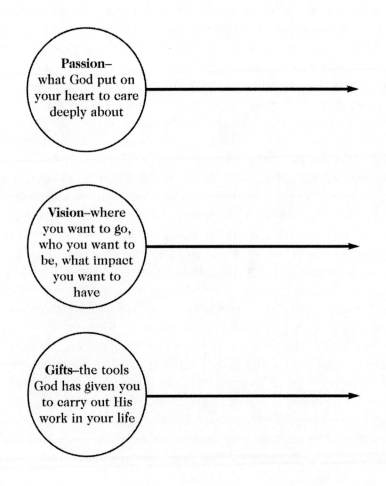

Living the Abundant Life

This seems to be a life that could be in balance, one apparently on the road to abundance. Passion, Vision, and Gifts have been discovered and are all generating energy, propelling this person forward. To the outside observer, it appears as if all of the elements of abundance are working in concert instead of against each other. as we have seen in previous examples.

What then is the problem? The problem is there is never a point where the lines – the vectors, the energy, the missions created from the separate elements of abundance – come together. With Passion, Vision, and Gifts aligned in this manner, you could express all of the elements and still be living separate lives. You could still be living with masks on, using a different face or a different element of abundance wherever you happen to be at the moment.

At work you could use your Vision, because it is most clearly defined there. At home you could employ your Passion. At church you could use your Gifts, because that is where it is easiest and safest to use them. It all makes sense except for one small matter – such is not the road to abundance. If we use the elements of abundance in this manner, we probably were not effective in truly communicating with God as we tried to discover the God-inspired Passion, the God-ordained Vision, and the spiritual Gifts He has bestowed upon us.

God wants us to live joy-filled, abundant lives on a full time basis. Those Gifts, those Passions, that Vision He bestowed upon us are meant to impact our lives every moment of every day. Living in such a manner, we can be completely who we are on a full time basis. Mask-free living, living for God, allows us to say about everything we do, "What I do is me. For this I came." But how do we get there and how does it look?

This is how the elements of abundance should work together to foster an environment where abundance can abound:

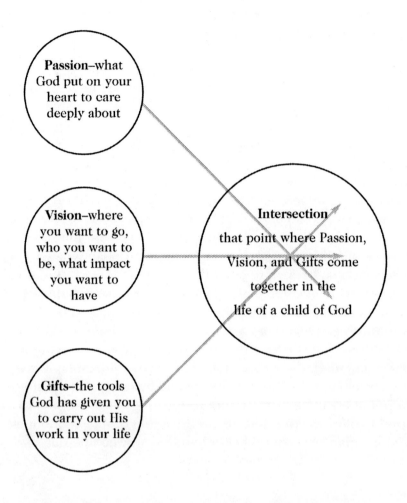

Passion gets your blood pressure up. Vision generates feelings of purpose as you strive toward the tomorrow you know you are supposed to live. Gifts give you confidence that you have been armed by the King for the work you are to do. The Intersection entails taking all of these elements and ensuring they come together on a consistent basis in your life. The Intersection means finding that point, those points, where you are feeding your Passion in a manner that works toward your Vision while fully employing your Gifts. That is the Intersection.

When you find your Intersection, you will experience what

Living the Abundant Life

can best be described as "coming home." When you find the Intersection, you will have identified what it is that combines your Passion, your Vision, and your Gifts in a manner that glorifies God and fulfills His purpose for your life. The feeling, the comfort, the peace that comes from finding that point may be likened to returning to that beloved home you left so many years ago, and discovering the most treasured of childhood memories. Moments like that are more than reminiscing. They are falling back and resting in the delight and the goodness of the memories. You are transformed to another place and time, and give in to that transformation willingly, restfully, and joyfully.

At the Intersection you rest in the peace, comfort, and sense of fulfillment that come from knowing you are doing exactly what God called you to do in your Faith, Family, and Vocation. Though there is a tomorrow – a distant future – in the elements of abundance, the Intersection means that you may rightfully claim at that very moment "What I do is me. For this I came." The Intersection is that thing or those things you can do, no matter how small or large, that will make you walk away saying, "That is why I am here. I am fulfilled and God is glorified by this. My life is worth it, if only because I was able to have that impact." It is all about today, right now, at the Intersection – and it is enough.

This brings us back to the introduction of this chapter: General McClellan's failures, the executives who live at 20,000 feet, and the recommendation that we move back and forth from the balcony to the dance floor. The Intersection is the ultimate weapon against spending too much time at the high altitudes. It is also effective in reminding us to move off the dance floor so we can gain clarity about what is important or unimportant relative to our Kingdom work.

The checks and balances that come from living at the Intersection could go something like this:

Is my Passion hot?
   Is my Burden linked to my Passion?
    Is my Vision clear?
     Do I know where God wants me to go?
     Do I understand my Gifts?
     So what?

At the end of the day, the Intersection demands to know what you are going to do with these separate elements of abundance. How will they come together and what impact will they have in your Faith, Family, and Vocation? The Intersection should bring the elements of abundance to a point. That point should be applicable in the different areas of life. Each day the Intersection demands to know what you will do with what God put on your heart to do. What will you do with it today? That is the question the Intersection poses.

You see, we have too many balcony dwellers and too many that are stuck on the dance floor. People live their lives at the dance floor level until they become so broken and disillusioned that they reach for something else. Finding in Jesus what they were missing, they accept His sacrifice and commit their lives to Him.

But that person still has to go to work the next day. He or she still has to deal with the family situations that were there before accepting Jesus. Jesus, the ultimate healer, the ultimate in living out the will of the Father, wants us to take what He has given us – Passion (Burden), Vision, and Gifts – and incorporate them into the fabric of every moment of our life. He wants us to do more than know Him and what He has given us. This was illustrated in Luke 6:46 (NIV) when Jesus asked "Why do you call me 'Lord, Lord' and do not do what I say?" In addition to knowing Him, we are also to follow Him and use what He has given us in accordance with His design.

The Intersection is where we must live if we are to truly be "more than conquerors" in everything we do. The Intersection is a result of the merger between the elements of abundance. In essence, it represents a merger between who God designed us to be and our daily routine – our calendar. The Intersection transforms the theoretical into present reality as we do the Kingdom work we were designed for on a full-time basis. The Intersection is that point where Jesus truly becomes real in our life and is represented in everything we do and say. In this condition we can truly be who we are and enjoy mask-free living.

I don't know if the road to abundance is a circular one, but I do know this. The road to abundance goes through the Intersection over and over and over again. It keeps the Passion, Vision, and Gifts real and relevant in our life on a daily basis. In many ways it keeps God relevant in our lives as we are reminded that, while God is a big God, He is also in every detail and wants us to live His promises, live in His will, and have His abundance, every moment of every day.

DISCOVERING MY INTERSECTION

The process described in this book is one of searching. Searching for abundance indeed, but before you answer the question of abundance, you must first figure out who you are to begin with. It is only from that basis that you can strive for the abundance that should mark your life as a child of the King.

I began my search because I was much more successful in everyone else's eyes than in my own. I had always been consistent with my smile and my laugh. I had a positive disposition, but I was starting to have to force it more than usual. As I looked at my life, there seemed to be nothing missing. I had an incredible marriage, great children, a career that I enjoyed, and a church that fed the spiritual needs of our family.

I discovered that I was missing the clearly defined Passion, Vision, and Gifts that constitute the first three elements of abundance. I had a great life, but had really just happened into it by virtue of having a great attitude about life. What I was sensing was what I believe God puts within each of us when we start feeling fulfilled by something other than Him. God put that deep nagging within me, that inescapable feeling that there was something more out there. It was only when I started dealing with those feelings that I began the journey to abundance.

I finally said, "I am happy. I have a great life. I am thankful for what I have, but I am not living as I should be. I am not living a fulfilled, joy-filled life. I do not have the abundance I am supposed to have as a Christ follower. I am not going anywhere until I find out how to live that kind of life. Help me, God, to find out how to live that way. Help me, God, to find out what it is that You want me to do with my life."

This conversation was the beginning of my journey toward the abundant life. The first element of abundance for me came relatively easily. It was not hard to discover that my Passion was leadership and connecting with and lifting people. A much longer period of introspection helped me realize that my Burden, forever linked to my Passion, is "the lack of victory, joy, and significance in the life of God's children." It again took some time for me to understand my Vision as I tried to wade through the esoteric world that we sometimes make Vision out to be. Eventually I realized that my Vision was simple but broad: helping "children of the King live out their John 10:10 inheritance." My Gifts were not difficult to determine. I prayed, studied, reflected, and looked at those things I enjoyed doing that brought me fulfillment. I knew what I was wired by God to do. I discerned that my Gifts were Leadership, Encouragement, and Teaching.

I cannot fully describe the feelings that accompanied my discovering these things about myself and about my relationship with God. All of a sudden, I felt closer to God than ever before. I realized that I was to live for Him and work with Him every day of my life. I will always remember this as the most critical period in my life.

As important as this period was, it was not without frustration. In fact, I was probably more frustrated than I had ever been in my life. Make no mistake about it, when you start getting serious about living out the will of God for your life, He will begin to transform you into the most powerful force on earth for carrying out that will. The flip side is that all of the forces aligned against God will come out of the woodwork and do everything possible to convince you that you are not what God has promised you are. Jesus illustrated this in Luke 11:24-26 (NLT) when He said:

> *When an evil spirit leaves a person, it goes into the
> desert, searching for rest. But when it finds none, it says,
> 'I will return to the person I came from.' So it returns
> and finds that its former home is all swept and clean.
> Then the spirit finds seven other spirits more evil than
> itself, and they all enter the person and live there. And so
> that person is worse off than before.*

Do not be surprised when you have to battle the frustration,
the lack of clarity, the criticism of people who say you are
wasting your time. You may have to fight through the noise of
those who suggest that you need to come back to the real world,
and the sounds from people who knowingly or unknowingly try
to get you to settle for mediocrity. This journey is not an easy
one. You will have to stay focused and on task while ensuring
you do not listen to well-intentioned, but misguided, advisors.
More critical, perhaps, is realizing there is a spiritual component
to the journey and the evil one would love nothing more than to
make you doubt that you have been designed for Kingdom work.

My journey fit all of the above. One of the things I did not
expect, though, was my reaction to discovering my Passion,
Vision, and Gifts. When I began to gain clarity about these
elements, I looked at my job and initially did not see how what
I was doing could possibly relate to what God was doing in my
life or how it related to abundance. I felt God doing things in
my life and bringing these new discoveries to me, but could
not comprehend where my new relationship with Him fit with
my role in corporate America.

What could I do? What was the answer? Where would I go?
What did God want me to do with my Passion, Vision, and
Gifts? Did He know I had a mortgage and a family complete
with many children and too many pets to support? How would
this work?

I began to think that using the first three elements of
abundance and having a true walk with God was somewhere
over the horizon. I thought I would do big things for God when

I achieved financial independence. I reasoned I could start doing more significant, meaningful things when I retired. I believed there was a certain net worth, or age, when I could shift from the rat race into doing something that would mean more and have lasting impact. The assumption was that there was a certain point that could be reached and then the switch could be flipped from insignificant to significant life pursuits. Again Jesus counseled me off this train of thought with a parable told in Luke 12:16-20 (NLT):

> Jesus said, "A rich man had a fertile farm that produced fine crops. In fact, his barns were full to overflowing. So he said, 'I know! I'll tear down my barns and build bigger ones. Then I'll have room enough to store everything. And I'll sit back and say to myself, My friend, you have enough stored away for years to come. Now take it easy! Eat, drink, and be merry!' But God said to him, 'You fool! You will die this very night. Then who will get it all?'"

From this it became readily apparent that I was not to wait until tomorrow to pursue a life of significance – there is no guarantee of a tomorrow. Another problem with waiting for tomorrow is the horizon tends to move as we try to move closer to it. The questions came much faster than answers but ultimately the Intersection provided the clarity I needed. I learned that the Intersection allows for tomorrow, but builds meaning, significance, and abundance into today. For me the Intersection simply represented combining the first three elements of abundance in a manner that allowed me to satisfy those elements on a day-by-day basis. My Intersection is as follows:

> Use LET (leadership, encouragement, and teaching – Gifts) to connect with and lift people, to build bigger people and better organizations, and to spread the message of abundance through word, deed, and example.

Living the Abundant Life

APPLYING MY INTERSECTION

For an Intersection to truly be the most important element of abundance, its relevance must be readily apparent. I knew the first three elements of abundance, but could not quite see how they would apply to all of the different areas of my life. The Intersection is what provided that clarity for me, particularly as it related to my vocation.

Instead of changing my career, I needed to focus my energy on those things that kept me walking in concert with what God wanted to do with my life. What I discovered was that it really did not matter so much what I was doing for a living. I no longer needed to find the perfect job in order to satisfy that stirring within me that knew there was more out there for my life. There is no perfect job. In fact, without a true relationship with God, there is no perfect church, there is no perfect home, there is no perfect spouse. There is a void in our life that God alone can fill. Our desire for perfection can only be satisfied when we are in relationship with the only perfect One. It is from this relationship that all good things in our life flow.

Before I found the elements of abundance, and particularly before I found the Intersection, I discovered that I was spending a great deal of time wondering – wondering if I was in the right career; wondering if I was in the right position; wondering if I was living in the right town; wondering if I was in the right salary range; wondering about all of the "ambient noise" in my life.

The Intersection took that wondering away. All of a sudden I looked anew at my employer and my career. Was everything as I wished it would be? Absolutely not – it never will be. But with my focus on the Intersection I asked if I could do the following in my current position: Could I "use LET (Gifts) to connect with and lift people, to build bigger people and better organizations, and to spread the message of abundance through word, deed, and example?"

The answer was astounding. Of course I could do those things. I was already doing some of them. What I found was that the necessary conditions for the Intersection were already in place. There were aspects of my job that truly filled my soul, though I did not realize it before. Some of the things I did tapped into my Passion, contributed to fulfilling my Vision, and employed my Gifts. There were even times when all of those things came together and allowed me to work at the Intersection, though it was a concept I was not familiar with at the time. There was really nothing missing.

The ultimate discovery was that in order for me to gain more job satisfaction, I needed only to prioritize more time and energy on activities that would entail my working at the Intersection which dealt with leading, encouraging, and teaching. So I built more of those activities into my schedule. I redoubled my efforts to do all three, because those things generated more than feelings of success, they generated feelings of significance. They were part of my Intersection, which involved spreading the message of abundance through word, deed, and example. I laced my leadership, my encouragement, and my teaching with discussions about living a balanced life. One of my favorite leadership quotes was attributed to Napoleon: "Leaders are dealers in hope." As a leader, I was positioned to deal in hope. I was right back at the Intersection.

I found that the Intersection was directly in front of me. I just needed to change the way I was looking at my career. It meant I had to choose to look at some things while not looking at others. For example, I chose not to pay as much attention to issues related to upward mobility. I no longer wanted to grab the next star heading north and make it to the top as quickly as possible. My goal was to live at the Intersection. It was there that I brought the best God gave me to the table. It was there that my influence was maximized. It was there that I experienced true feelings of significance whether I was promoted or not. It was at the Intersection that I experienced the vocational impact of the Biblical guidance to "be transformed by the renewing of your mind" (Rom 12:2 NIV). I didn't need to change my company, my job, or my location. I just needed to renew my mind and be transformed by doing so.

I chose not to look at the things that frustrated me. I chose

Living the Abundant Life

not to focus on them regardless of whether they were true or not, accurate or inaccurate. It didn't matter. If it helped me live and work at the Intersection, I focused on it. If it didn't help me live and work at the Intersection, I refused to focus on it. That is not an easy path, but it is a simple one. It is all about focus – focusing on the right things and consciously ignoring other things.

One point I might add for clarification is that the Intersection also kept me honest about what I fought for. Personally, I do not mind conflict and feel there is a need for open and honest conflict in most organizations. My problem was that I was always willing to square off against any Goliath who stood in my way if I felt I was in the right.

Understanding my Intersection helped me clarify what I should be fighting for. I did not have to oversee every engagement or win every battle. Sometimes you must have mercy on an adversary that you could crush, because doing so would not be in the best interest of the bigger picture. So, I learned to pick my battles. The apostle Paul did not say he fought just any fight. He fought the "good fight" (2 Tim 4:7).

I learned to recognize the difference between the "good fight" and "an available fight" and to discipline myself to only be involved in the former. Interestingly enough, this picking and choosing of the conflicts also meant I could be fearless in the battles and "charge the hill" no matter the odds or cost.

In doing our Kingdom work, perhaps we should all remember Stonewall Jackson's response to a reporter's question about his utter fearlessness and bravery on the battlefield. Stonewall replied, "My religious belief teaches me to feel as safe in battle as in bed. God has fixed the time for my death. I do not concern myself about that, but to always be ready, no matter when it may overtake me."

When you know what you believe in and what you are called by God to do, you will be less apt to take offense and more conditioned to fight the "good fight."

Living at the Intersection, I also chose not to worry so much about whose approval I had and who did not approve of what I was doing. That is not to say I disregarded the opinion of others. It is too easy for that to develop into a callous disdain for people in general. I did not want that. So I listened patiently to the dull, the clueless, the unkind, and the misinformed alongside those who really cared and helped with my journey.

But while I listened I also realized that in the end, my Faith, my Family, and my Vocation are between me and God. First and foremost, I must maintain my daily, moment-by-moment focus on Him and on ensuring that I am living the life that He would have me live. I am convinced that we sometimes cannot see God clearly because we are unable to see past those people standing between us and Him. I regard everyone in a positive manner, but primarily keep counsel with an audience of One – God. If I am at the Intersection, I have convergence between me and the things He wants me to do with my life every day.

What does this convergence look like? What day-to-day activities represent the Intersection in my life? How do Passion, Vision, and Gifts come together in the life of this child of God?

I believe I am at the Intersection when:

- I pray for and with my children every night and speak God's truth into their life, so they will grow up convinced that God loves them and that He wants to do amazing things through their lives.
- I encourage my wife to pursue what God put on her heart to do whenever He puts it there.
- I teach leadership in my work organization in such a way that children of the King come to recognize their unique ability to influence both performance and the lives of those placed in their care.
- I coach and encourage people to hold fast to their vision, despite what the world may be telling them.
- I convince people that the values they love on Sunday can come to work with them; that they do not have to wear masks at work.
- I build an organization that achieves success and helps

those in the organization grow toward whatever they are wired by God to be.

- I work with groups at church on maximizing their leadership potential and using their Gifts in Faith, Family, and Vocation.
- I bow before each meal, no matter where I am, providing comfort and modeling to someone that it is acceptable to be an avowed, admitted Christ follower.
- I help people realize that a life of abundance could and should be theirs by virtue of their being a child of the King.
- I help someone understand that their career decisions can and should be oriented around their Passion, Burden, Vision, and Gifts – that it is acceptable to say "yes" or "no" based on what God is telling them to do with their lives.
- I give a speech, teach a class, or write a book whether I feel qualified to do so or not, if my relationship with God leads me to believe that these things are what He wants me to do.

The results of my time at the Intersection are up to God and for God. God is God and I am not. I am content to remain at the Intersection where I can work with and for Him. It is enough. But in order to walk along the path of abundance and live at the Intersection, I had to lay the preparatory groundwork for the transformation. I had to discover the first three elements of abundance.

This is so important because I would never have recognized my Intersection, my sweet spot, had I not studiously and prayerfully discovered, then integrated, my Passion, Vision, and Gifts in a manner that offered me a glimpse of what the Intersection could look like. In providing me this snapshot, He gave me a guide to follow to ensure my labors were consistent with His designs for my life.

What does that guide tell me to do? It tells me to "use LET (Gifts) to connect with and lift people, to build bigger people and better organizations, and to spread the message of abundance through word, deed, and example." It really is as simple as that. Every day, at the Intersection, responding to the call – that is abundance.

THE INTERSECTION — THE IMPACT

The Intersection is so important in the quest for the abundant life because it constantly reinforces our impact as children of the King. Why is this reinforcement so needed? It constantly reminds us of who we are and why we are here.

How many of us have left the church service inspired, only to forget what the sermon was about by the time we finished our afternoon nap? How many of us have wondered where our connection with God went when it is Thursday and it seems as though the lunacy of the work week will never end? How many of us have heard people speak of doing great things and quietly wondered why we never felt that way? We see their Passion, we see their focus, we see their commitment, and silently we wonder why we do not feel that way ourselves.

Deep inside we want to. We yearn to. We want to feel that Passion surging within us. We want to remember what it feels like to get caught up in the flow of something we consider to be good, meaningful, even worth sacrificing for. We want to feel like we matter and that our lives count. But we do not know how to bring that into reality. We do not know how to make those thoughts (captured on Sunday, revived in morning Bible studies, renewed in our small group sessions) become translated into actions that will provide meaning in our day-to-day lives. I speak with so many people who believe "in principle" that God put them on the face of the earth to do something for Him. It is Biblical, so these good people are always ready to accept that God has a plan for their lives.

The details of that plan are beyond them though. They stopped looking years ago. Once upon a time, they believed there was something they were designed to do because the Bible tells them so, but they don't believe it enough to change the way they look at life. They believe, but they settle. In a way they are like the man who said to Jesus, "Lord, I believe;

Living the Abundant Life

help my unbelief" (Mk 9:24). Tragically, some are not even asking for help anymore.

So often we get caught in the trap of thinking that we will only be happy when …. We think that success, significance, happiness, joy, and satisfaction will be provided when some future event occurs or a milestone is reached. Such artificial markers of success serve only to tantalize us as we go through life. We strive so hard to reach them and once we have arrived we realize that the fruits of our labor simply do not satisfy us. We reflect on the journey and one day reach the point where we are worn out, dissatisfied, and disillusioned. So we settle into the sad state where we just don't ask so much from life.

The Intersection reminds us that we are special and are called by God to do certain things while on the face of the earth. At the top of the list is to surrender control of our lives to Him, follow Him, live joy-filled lives, lives without fear, lives as more than conquerors, lives of abundance.

In our discussion of abundance in an earlier chapter, I identified a significant characteristic of abundance: Abundance is about living today, right now, to its fullest and in the direction of your God-ordained purpose in life. The Intersection serves us so well because it provides a consistent schedule of reinforcement rather than the promise of a pot of gold at the end of the rainbow. The dream of that pot of gold will simply not sustain us through the peaks and valleys of life.

I received this reinforcement from the Intersection as I wrote this chapter. I had to deal with an extremely difficult, even painful, situation at work. The unsatisfactory resolution to this event left me feeling completely exhausted when I finally made it home. After spending some time with my children, time in which I could enjoy something again yet wind down and just be truly exhausted, a thought hit me. I pulled out my Bible and reviewed two sheets of paper which are taped to the inside cover. Among other things, on those sheets of paper are the following questions and definitions:

- Did I tap into my Passion today? (Passion –
  Leadership; connecting with and lifting people.)

- Did my Passion relate to my Burden? (Burden – The lack of victory, joy, and significance in the life of God's children.)
- Who was glorified, God or me?
- Did I use my Gifts today? (Gifts – Leadership, encouragement, teaching.)
- Did I make a conscious effort to grow in my area of giftedness today?
- Did I see today clearly, while maintaining my Vision for what tomorrow could and should be? (Vision – children of the King living out their John 10:10 inheritance.)
- Did I spend time at the Intersection today? (Intersection – Use LET to connect with and lift people, to build bigger people and better organizations, and to spread the message of abundance through word, deed, and example.)
- Who was glorified, God or me?

The list serves as my abundance check. After an extraordinarily difficult day full of pain, struggle, and sacrifice, I needed to be reminded of who I was and why I even wanted to be in the game. I wanted rest. I wanted to settle. I wanted my phone to not ring. I wanted to have no appointments and no one-on-one's and to not feel the need to encourage or lift or do anything. I wanted to be tired, I wanted to sit down, I wanted a temporary reprieve, I wanted a break, I wanted an escape.

My reprieve did not come from rest; it came in the form of the questions cited above. My rest came from the reminder of who I am, why I am here, and from the certainty that my perception is based on prayer, study, reflection, and the working of God in my life. No matter how tired, worn out, or beaten down I was, I realized that I was acting on orders from the Master. Nothing can stop me from my appointed rounds – not tragedy, not circumstance, not difficulties, not adverse dispositions, not even temporary setbacks. To the world that tries its best to pull us down, I was able to respond with the words of Nehemiah: "I am doing a great work and I cannot come down" (Neh 6:3 NASB).

I am doing a great work because I am at the Intersection. I am doing a great work because being at the Intersection reinforces, every day, that I am walking in God's will. Living at the Intersection reminds me that I serve an active God, One who is not distant, but near at hand, working in my life each day, leading me into a closer relationship with Him.

Desirous of conveying the abundant life that Jesus came to provide, He keeps beckoning us to follow Him so we might experience His joy. Living and working at the Intersection is, in essence, following Him. It entails identifying those points where Passion, Vision, and Gifts come together, and maintaining our focus on those critical points. We are such special beings. Created in the image of God, we possess, by birthright, incredible abilities and direct tasking from the King of kings. But our ability to execute the plan for our life, to truly be co-workers with God, may hinge on our success at filtering out the ambient noise and focusing on those frequencies that ring true.

Living and working at the Intersection is one of the most important things we can do to keep the main thing in life the main thing. Even our best of intentions are frequently replaced by those small things that bombard our attention and command a few minutes of our time. Pretty soon we don't have a few minutes. Eventually we assume that getting a few minutes of free time is the goal. A few minutes of peace and quiet is not the goal, it cannot be. Living at the Intersection though, where you are in touch with what God put on your heart and called you to do, may indeed be a worthy goal.

Discovering your Intersection is paramount to abundance. The Intersection transforms those higher level thoughts and aspirations we gain from church, life, reflection, and prayer, into concrete steps we can take every day in order to do Kingdom work and live an abundant life.

PERSONAL REFLECTIONS

■

What is your Passion?

What is your Burden?

What is your Vision?

What are your Gifts?

The Intersection is that point where Passion, Vision, and Gifts come together in the life of a child of God. Try writing your Passion, Burden, Vision, and Gifts into a statement describing what you might be doing when those elements intersect. *For example, in my case, my Intersection is: Use LET (Gifts) to connect with and lift people (Burden and Passion), to build bigger people and better organizations (Passion) and to spread the message (Gifts) of abundance (Burden and Vision) through word, deed, and example.*

What is your Intersection?

Describe how you could use your Intersection statement in your Vocation? List 3 things you could do in your Vocation where you would be at the Intersection.

Describe how you could use your Intersection statement in your Faith? List 3 things you could do in your Faith walk where you would be at the Intersection.

Describe how you could use your Intersection statement in your Family? List 3 things you could do with your Family where you would be at the Intersection.

7

LIVING THE
ABUNDANT LIFE

Why are we here? What does all of this amount to? The peaks seem so high and the valleys so low sometimes. We would like to think it all amounts to something of significance. It does. It is accurate and Biblically sound to say that we are here "to glorify God." And the older we get, the wiser we seem when we give this response to the question of life.

But too often we wonder: How do I do that? How do I glorify God? I'm a banker, or a broker, or a teacher, or a lawyer, or a salesman. How can I glorify God when this is what I do for a living?

Many of us would have to admit that the concept of spending our life "glorifying God" might not seem too exciting. What would it entail? Does it mean muting all external displays of emotion so the world would believe we are a rock of faith, unfazed by the toils and tribulations of the day? Does it mean committing to a life of poverty so that there can be no question of our priorities in life? Could it mean rejecting the pursuit of "worldly" goals such as promotions, increased responsibility, increased salary, and incentive pay-outs? The answer to these questions is an emphatic no – these are not the ways that we glorify God.

The truth of the matter is, we glorify God by committing all things to Him. We glorify God by doing our work as if we are working for God, not man (Colossians 3:23). God loved us first

– we glorify Him by loving Him back. We glorify God by pursuing a relationship with Him incessantly. Through that relationship our actions will flow in a manner that honors Him. We glorify God by not wasting what He has given us. We glorify God by truly living life and not just sucking air, so that we will reflect the image of the One who created and loves us.

We glorify God by believing *in* Him and *believing* Him; believing that we are His most cherished creation; believing He wants us to live in relationship with Him; believing He wants us to live victorious, joy filled and abundant lives. If we really believe these things, we cannot possibly live as if we were defeated, lost orphans. We are children of the King, and children of the King must live as royalty – because the King's authority is legitimate.

In order to live in this manner we must commit to the life that Jesus came to provide. In John 10:10 He said, "I have come that they may have life, and that they may have it more abundantly." To live as He prescribed we must live the abundant life.

THE ELEMENTS OF ABUNDANCE

We must know the Passion that God placed on our heart. We serve a God of passion who has a particular zeal for us, His children. We are created in His image. It naturally follows that we would be wired as passionate beings. Our Passion represents the fingerprints of God on our soul. Though we care about other things, our Passion is what keeps us up at night; it is what elevates our blood pressure for all the right reasons; it is what keeps us engaged; it is what keeps us from getting bored with the task; it is what inspires us and gives us hope that tomorrow will have meaning.

It is worth repeating Jean de la Fontaine's powerful insight: "Man is so made that when anything fuels his soul, impossibilities vanish." Passion makes us live out this statement and gives us reason to keep going. Amidst the emptiness of life it fills us, it warms us, it comforts us. It provides the positive discontent to keep pushing forward. We desperately need it lest

Living the Abundant Life

we sink into the dull routine that life will always become when lived apart from our God-inspired Passions.

But Passion has a dark side, you will remember. Unbridled or misdirected Passion can be traced to virtually every vice or sin that one might imagine: illicit sex, drugs, alcohol, violence – all deviant versions of Passion. Add to that list workaholism; lives driven by the need to accumulate wealth and possessions that will only fade away; seemingly harmless hobbies that take so much time and focus away from our Faith and Family. A list of the negative by-products of misdirected passion would be virtually endless.

Those of us who seek to follow Jesus and live the abundant life must not only find our Passion, but harness it as well. We do this by applying a Godly burden to our Passion. Jesus said, "If any of you wants to be my follower, you must put aside your selfish ambition, shoulder your cross, and follow me" (Mt 16:24 NLT). Carrying our cross and shouldering our burden will ensure that the Passion which inspires us will always do so in the direction of God.

We must know the God-ordained Vision that helps us determine what we are to do with our Passion. God tells us in the Bible that we are His workmanship, His fellow workers, and that there are things He wants to accomplish in and through our life. As we identify our God-ordained Vision, we also incorporate the Destination for our journey, the Ideal Self or person we want to be when we get there, and the Impact we are to have on this world and the next.

The Bible teaches that each of us in relationship with Jesus has been given a spiritual Gift. Knowing what our Gifts are means gaining a fuller understanding of how we achieve our Vision – how we fit individually into the Kingdom drama that is unfolding. The Kingdom work God has called us to perform is accomplished using the tools and implements (the Gifts) that He has provided. Learning, using, and developing these Gifts enables God's generosity to flow through us.

Finally, the Intersection represents taking all of the other

Elements of Abundance – Passion with a Godly Burden, Vision, and Gifts – and ensuring that they come together in our life on a routine basis. In so doing, we are able to take the lofty thoughts and ideals represented by the other Elements of Abundance and use them on a daily basis.

Living at the Intersection, I am able to find something in each day that allows me to say that I am doing Kingdom work. Does it fully accomplish my Vision or satisfy my Passion? Of course not. If the source of my Passion and Vision is God, then my Passion and Vision will never be fully satisfied while I'm here on earth.

But living at the Intersection does provide me with the satisfaction of knowing that while I'm on earth, I'm walking and working hand-in-hand with the King. At the Intersection, I look for God and the things He has called me to do every single day. Everything in the drama of life is viewed against the backdrop of God. Living at the Intersection also provides me with the comfort of knowing that if my life ended today, I would stand before God ready to report that I tried every day to use what He gave me to carry out the work that He put me here to do.

At the Intersection is where I can see those opportunities the best. It is where I can see God at work and feel my relationship with Him the most. At the Intersection is where I can walk and work in the will and pleasure of God and say, at the end of the day, "It is enough. If this were all I was called to do, this would indeed be enough." The Intersection provides that each day.

Living at the Intersection means we live an integrated life. Who we are and what we do merge so we are able to say: "What I do is me. For this I came." In addition, we live as children of the King. We were made in His image and designed to live in relationship with Him. In that noble line, we were created with designs of grandeur and wiring that fits us for Kingdom work. The Spirit that hovered over the face of the earth when the world was being created is inside of you and me. The Spirit that strengthened Moses, steeled Peter's nerves, emboldened Stephen, sustained Paul, and ministered to Jesus

Living the Abundant Life

after his 40 days in the desert lives inside of us – the Christ followers. What that Spirit desires to do in and through us is nothing less than He did in and through the saints of old. It is the same Spirit, same God, and same transformation.

In order to achieve this transformation, we must condition ourselves to become more fully aware of God's full time work in our life and our full time role in building His Kingdom. Living at the Intersection reminds us of these things and enables us to receive the constant reinforcement and affirmation that comes with knowing we are important parts of what God is doing in this world and in preparing for the next. Our life does matter.

SIX FACTORS THAT KEEP US FROM LIVING AN ABUNDANT LIFE

Even with our royal bloodline we often spend our lives in trivial, miniscule pursuits. We spend our precious time engaged in a myriad of hobbies and toys, quasi-passions and jobs, complaints and gossip, and dozens of other things that keep our focus off the incredible, life-changing, Kingdom-impacting work we were put here to do. Why do we forget that we were made in His image? Why do we neglect the gifts He has given us? Why do we focus on everything that distracts us while turning down the volume on the Godly passions He placed on our hearts? Why don't we believe *and* live our lives accordingly?

The following distractions and deceptions can keep us from living the abundant life. These factors are:

Ambient Noise – There is so much noise in our life that we find it hard to hear those sounds that ring true with our soul. Amidst all of the activity, it is possible to lose the ability to discern the voice of God calling to us and beckoning us to Him. We miss opportunities to fulfill our life's purpose by living in relationship with Him and doing something of significance for the King. We have to find a way to turn down the noise and focus on those truer frequencies that will make our life count.

Lack of Modeling – We might push harder to become everything we should be if we had more examples of others doing the same. When we get ready to step out on the limb and really have an impact on this world, we pause just long enough to wonder if we will be out there all by ourselves.

The answer is yes – and no. Sometimes it feels like we are out there on our own. But in the midst of this loneliness, you will find fellow sojourners. Build relationships with them, seek mentoring as appropriate, find ways to be around them and take advantage of the encouragement and guidance that comes from anyone trying to live an abundant life. Be sure to identify role models in all three areas of life – Faith, Family, and Vocation.

Fear of Rejection – We fear rejection from those who love us, from those who dislike us, and even from those who don't know us. The smallest of people and minds can squelch the biggest of dreams with one critical comment. It should not be this way – it must not!

Instead, we must grow to accept the fact that if we are casting a significant vision, a God-ordained Vision, then that Vision may not be embraced by many and will be rejected outright by others. Look at the visionaries who established a different standard. You can find them in any walk of life. They are ridiculed by peers, rebuked by critics, questioned by those who support them, and sometimes even rejected by close friends and family members. Even Jesus experienced this when He began His ministry. He commented "But the truth is, no prophet is accepted in his own hometown" (Lk 4:24 NLT). Should we expect a different reaction?

A lack of acceptance by others does not mean that we are wrong or that we need to change our vision, our focus, or our plans. Nor does it mean that others are evil, deranged or just downright nasty – though some of them may be! It simply means we are casting a vision in the direction of the abundant life. For some reason, that makes many people very uncomfortable and they may feel the need to criticize or reject you. Let them have their say, pull out any small kernels of wisdom and truth that usually accompany such feedback, and thank them for their time and input. Then throw the conversation out of your mind and run like the wind from those "ankle grabbers" who try to pull you back down to earth as you are floating off in the direction of your dreams. Just press on!

Fear in General – We live in a generalized state of fear as we look at our dreams and wonder if we can really do it. We wonder if people will question our motives. We fear the results of a true attempt at abundance that fails. We fear that we will fail, so we don't even try. Sometimes we try, fail, and then just write it off as a bad idea.

We must overcome the generalized condition of fear, as well as the fear of rejection, by recognizing the source of fear. There is a healthy fear that lets us know when danger is imminent. That is not the fear we are attacking. We are attacking the other forms of fear that cause us to pull up short from living the life we were intended to live. We must consider the source of those fears. Paul counseled Timothy on this subject by saying, "For God has not given us a spirit of fear, but of power and of love and of a sound mind" (2 Tim 1:7). If God is not the author of fear then who is?

Consider adopting the same commitment I made a number of years ago, that has helped me deal with the fear in my own life. My commitment was to "let nothing keep me from living a life of freedom. In particular, I resist and confront fear of anything as if it is trying to take away my very next breath."

This commitment serves as my reminder to fight the good fight, to fight the fear that is not of God and can have no good purpose in my life. No matter who you are or where you are in your journey toward abundance, you will need something like this to sustain you in the on-going battle with fear. Be sure you are prepared!

Exhaustion – The pace of activities continues to elevate dramatically with no sign of decreasing as long as we are breathing. We sleepwalk through our days in such an exhausted condition that we have come to believe rest is the reward. We are overloaded with tasks and priorities. The battles of the past still weigh heavily on our minds. Our emotional baggage gets heavier and heavier. Instead of dragging it around we collapse where we are.

Settling – So we stay where we are, and in so doing, bargain with life. We propose to life that we will not push, strive, or stay out on the edge of the limb if it will not keep dealing with us so roughly. We settle for an existence that provides some stimulation, but rarely links it with our soul. We desperately want more out of life and cannot imagine why it's not dropped on our doorstep. We peer out the window of our soul, disappointed that we don't see the snow-capped peaks of abundance that used to inspire us so greatly. And we imagine that everything would be all right if we could only have that daily dose of inspiration.

All the while we forget that we are the ones who moved away from the mountain. We decided that the journey was too difficult, that the consistent need for caution and the occasional fall outweighed the benefits of the daily doses of inspiration. At some point we decided that we were no longer willing to pay the price. We settled for less.

We grow tired of being attacked about every decision, of people taking shots at us, of doing great things only to fall down the next day. We grow tired of naysayers who have never climbed, but claim to be experts at critiquing our journey. So we stop searching for the abundant life that Jesus came that we might have. But we don't stop wondering and we don't stop wandering. And try as we may, we cannot get rid of that deep gnawing within us that cries out, "This is not all that I am here for."

These factors can cause us to lose focus on the quest for abundance. We are bombarded by the noise of life, the lack of modeling, the fear of rejection, the generalized fear, and the exhaustion. Eventually we settle for far less than we should. But we cannot find peace or fulfillment in such mediocrity. There is something within us that knows we are wired to be and do more.

ABUNDANT LIVING AND WHAT IT LOOKS LIKE

The factors described above work to keep us from living the life we should. An awareness of these factors is critical because this is more than an issue of self-discipline or wasted human capacity. We all have a host of "what if" scenarios that have affected our lives. What if I had taken that job? What if I had tried a little harder? What if I had done this or not done that? What if ...? What if ...? What if ...?

What we are trying to address is a much more significant "what if" scenario. We are trying to avoid saying "what if" at the end of our life and have the question pertain to the truly important things in life: What if I had tried to do what God wired me to do? What if I had taken the time to reflect on just what my life meant and the impact I was supposed to have on the world? What if I had really tried to do something significant? What if I had tried, even failed? Would that make me feel more complete? What if I had really lived out my priorities?

This is not an issue of Heaven or hell, by the way. This is an issue of living or not living as we were designed to live. This is an issue of ensuring that when our journey is complete, we don't have "I wish I had tried" on our list of regrets.

Jesus said, "I have come that they may have life, and that they may have it more abundantly" (Jn 10:10). You do not have to live an abundant life to get into Heaven. But it seems logical that we would identify abundance as one of our primary life goals and pursue it with all we have. If Jesus came so we would have abundance, then it makes sense for those of us who follow Him to strive for it. There is no reason for people destined for Heaven to spend their human existence in a defeated condition that feels more like hell. Instead we should choose abundance. The characteristics of the abundant life are as follows:

Abundance is mask-free living. We cannot live the abundant life, where joy overflows, if there is constant war being waged between the major components of our life – Faith, Family, and Vocation. As we have already discussed, there must be consistency between the different components of our life and they must be complimentary. Living this way will enable us to walk freely in the different areas of life, in our different roles, but be who we are in each of those roles. In doing this we drop the masks and become one person – the same person – in all of the different roles.

Abundance is determining that the abundant life is your birthright. The only way you can approach life in such a manner is to become convinced that abundance is your birthright. Being convinced of this means that we get to the point where we can state that, as a Christ follower, if Jesus came so that we would have abundance, then we shall have it – period!

Abundance then becomes not a destination or something we hope for; it becomes a part of who we are and something that we enjoy each day. The abundant life becomes our expectation and the norm because it is our right, our birthright, as fully devoted, fully surrendered Christ followers.

Living the abundant life requires that our life be transformed from the inside out by the working of the Holy Spirit. Living the abundant life requires that we accept the grace, love, and redemption offered to us at so great a cost. But living the abundant life also requires that we make the determination to live the abundant life by accepting that it is our birthright. We will settle for nothing less.

Abundance is doing what God wired you to do. Abundant living means that you and I are finally doing what God wired us to do. When we start doing what God wired us to do and move away from things not related to our wiring, our days will take on new meaning. The excitement and confidence of going through a day knowing that you are doing what God wired you to do is absolutely incredible. The feeling of impact, of significance, and of having a personal and lasting influence on the world around you every day will cause you to get more and more committed to living life based on this wiring that God has provided.

Perhaps the single most important factor of abundance as it relates to God's wiring is this: You have to believe that you have been uniquely wired, uniquely gifted, by the God who makes no mistakes. You have to believe that you are no coincidence and that you did not arrive where you are by chance.

Abundance is about living today, right now, to its fullest and in the direction of your God-ordained purpose in life. It is a paradoxical existence when you start living the abundant life. Everything has to be right now, but your "right now" takes

Living the Abundant Life

on a Kingdom perspective. You demand your daily dose of significance. You refuse to let a day go by without doing something related to your purpose for being. You will not wait any longer on the abundant life or living your dream.

You don't fall into depression and give up hope if you are not able to achieve your dream today. If you came one step closer and made one realization that will help you get there, or grew in an area crucial to the accomplishment of your mission, you regard it as a day of abundance. Instead of seeing the distance left to travel you see that you are closer today than yesterday, and this realization convinces your psyche of the undeniability of your mission.

Linking your goal to God's purpose for your life ensures that you will always have a mission which will involve challenge, growth, risk, and trials, but most of all significance. This is critical because more than anything, we all want to feel like our life matters, that we make a difference. Abundance is about living today, right now, to its fullest and in the direction of your God-ordained purpose in life.

Abundance is accompanied by high energy levels. A natural outgrowth or reflection of abundance in our lives is energy. If you are doing what you are wired to do and moving toward your purpose for being, there will be a clearly identifiable extra bounce in your step.

Abundant living and energy will always have a high degree of correlation. If you are living an abundant life you will have an energy output equal to the task of abundance. The reason for this unlimited wellspring of energy in the abundant life is, quite simply, the source. Jesus told the woman at the well: "People soon become thirsty again after drinking this water. But the water I give them takes away thirst altogether. It becomes a perpetual spring within them, giving them eternal life" (Jn 4:13 NLT).

Our search for significance always leaves us feeling thirsty again, no matter how deeply we drink from the wells of life. Apart from God, we cannot be filled, our thirst cannot be quenched. Jesus offers living water that "takes away thirst altogether" and "becomes a perpetual spring within them."

This perpetual spring is why energy must be reflected in abundant living. If we are living an abundant life, we have a perpetual spring of life within us. This stream never stops. It always flows, providing life-giving, life-rejuvenating sustenance. The amazing thing about this perpetual spring is that the source of the stream is within us. It gives life and eliminates the need for dependence on outside sources for abundance.

If you have tapped into this source within you, an outflow of energy will naturally become part of your countenance. Just as dams use the power of water to create copious amounts of energy, so the streams of living water flowing within us produce energy that naturally emanates from us. So the presence of abundance will always be accompanied by a high level of energy.

The natural result of such a condition is that you will be continually refreshed by a virtually endless supply of energy, evident in everything from your talk to your walk to the gleam in your eye, as the source of your abundance moves from external and changing sources to the streams of living water that emanate from within you.

Abundance changes your definition of success. Abundant living brings to life more success than you might ever have imagined. Abundant living, though, ushers in goals that are unchanging and Kingdom-oriented rather than fleeting and transitory. When you approach your goals and your life from the basis of your divine wiring and what God put you here to do, there will be a consistency about your actions and orientation that will carry you for the rest of your life. No longer will you be dependent upon success measures that you adopt from the rest of the world. Instead, you adopt measures of success based on your relationship with God. These measures will encompass all of the different Faith, Family, and Vocational changes and challenges that you are subjected to. You have to choose if you will spend or invest your time and how you will judge the outcome or success of your efforts: by lasting, eternal, Kingdom standards or your own limited versions of success and significance? The choice is yours.

Abundance wins the routine battle with fear. When you live the abundant life that Jesus came that you might have, the element of fear does not disappear. But the abundant life changes the way you approach fear and its impact on your life and decisions. Since fear will be with you no matter what, you must decide to confront it daily and ensure that it does not become a major determinant in your decision-making process. Fear will try to get you to give up but you cannot – you must not.

You must see fear for what it is and heed what fear is trying to tell you, without letting it stop you from doing what must be done. God is counting on your willingness and ability to conquer fear, and on your striving toward abundance, toward Him and His purposes, each day. "And we know that all things work together for good to those who love God, to those who are called according to His purpose" (Rom 8:28). This promise tells you that there is meaning in everything you do and that God is building you through every event or circumstance. "All things work together for good ..." as long as our purposes are in line with His.

Your confidence in your God-ordained purpose in life will increase every time you overcome the immobilizing effects of fear and step out in faith. Remember – abundance and fear cannot co-exist as equals. Abundance must consistently confront and quiet your fears if it is to continue to grow and thrive in your life.

Abundance is about victory but comes only after surrender. Abundance is about winning. It is about victory. Romans 8:37 (NIV) is so applicable to a life of abundance. It says: "In all these things we are more than conquerors through Him who loved us." But you cannot live the abundant life without surrendering your life. You cannot achieve victory unless you give up claim to yourself. You cannot become more than a conqueror until you have conquered yourself and put your life in the hands of the Master.

Surrender is when your entire perspective changes. Everything – every event, detail, and situation in your life is viewed and processed against the backdrop of God. Everything you do and everything you are is related to God.

Contrary to many opinions, surrender is not a passive process. Surrendering a life to God does not mean giving up control – quite the contrary. Surrender means controlling every moment of every day and ensuring that the direction of everything we do or say is toward God. Surrender means that we take every thought captive and make it obedient to Christ (2 Cor 10:5). We don't let go – we take everything captive – word, thought, and deed – and place it at the foot of the cross.

While He walked with us, Jesus said again and again, in various ways, "Follow me." That remains His message today. We have to listen for the voice of the Creator of the universe as He whispers our name and gives us the orders intended only for us.

Surrender means nothing less than saying "God is God and I am not. God is in control and I am not. God is the God of the universe and I officially and permanently declare myself unsuited for the task." As Louie Giglio said, "If God is 'I AM' then by definition 'I am not.'" Let God be God. With those declarations you are free to simply do whatever it is that He places in your heart to do at the very moment He says to do it.

Surrender means you acknowledge that God created you to have some kind of magnificent impact on this world, and that you are giving Him permission to use you to do amazing things for Him. Surrender means you are willing and ready to do "whatever" God wants you to do "whenever" He wants you to do it – no matter what. Surrender means you believe finding and living out His purpose for your life is your primary objective, and you will let nothing come between you and your objective.

Surrender means that the destination is not yours. It means that the speed of the journey is not yours. Surrender means that success or failure is not yours. Surrender means that you and I are simply doing what we are told to do by the Creator of the universe and that guidance is sufficient for us. God is God and I am not – and that's okay. You must say to Jesus about your life what Peter said to Him so long ago, "… because you say so, I will"(Lk 5:5 NIV).

Until you have this type of surrender, you cannot expect to

Living the Abundant Life

have a "more than conqueror" type of life. Abundance is about victory, but it is always preceded by surrender.

WHAT IS THE ALTERNATIVE TO THE LIFE WE HAVE BEEN LIVING?

The alternative to the life we may have been living is to realize that Jesus came so that we might have life and have it more abundantly. It is the determination that you will live an abundant life – no matter what. You decide that a good life today or a great life someday is not good enough. Instead you find an Intersection between your Passion, Burden, Vision, and Gifts – inspired and given to you by God – and commit that you will live at that Intersection, in abundance, every day of your life.

Once this occurs you can begin to experience mask-free living, when who you are remains constant in your Faith, Family, and Vocation.

You will stop thinking that abundance applies to someone else and accept it as your birthright as a believer.

You will feel the confidence that comes from doing – and knowing that you are doing – exactly what God wired you to do and to be.

You will walk in God's will for your life, knowing it will no longer be something that you do tomorrow, but will instead be satisfaction that you receive from today.

You will experience the high energy levels that come from tapping into streams of living water – from within!

You will find your definition of success is modified and placed in a more eternal, unchanging, and meaningful context.

You will routinely win in the battle with fear – even those fears that you alone know that you have.

You will understand the freedom that comes from giving up your claim to divinity. You give up trying to rule the world, even your own world, and let God be God. In so doing you take captive every thought, word, and deed and wrestle it to the cross, where it is submitted to Jesus for His guidance and direction.

Finally, you surrender to the One who made us and loves us more than we can imagine.

You are free to do what He tells you to do and make that incredible statement a true reflection of your life: "Because you say so, I will."

In this position of surrender, God is able to work in and through us and enable us to live the life that He desires for us. In living this abundant life we will glorify Him in all we do because it will all be about Him – our Faith, our Family, our Vocation – all are surrendered to Him. He is able to speak to and through us, and we are able to discern His guidance for our life.

In this condition, we find ourselves doing again and again what He tells us to do, and living in the warmth of His influence in our day-to-day existence. Living in such a manner brings us closer to God, closer to who we were meant to be, closer to living like true children of the King, closer to the victory, joy, and significance that should mark our lives. It brings us closer to making the statement our own: "What I do is me. For this I came."

"For this I came."

A NOTE TO
SMALL GROUPS

I have been taught and have experienced first hand that life change occurs in small groups. In small groups we feel again the bonds that community can form, particularly a community connected by the love of Jesus. Willow Creek church and the Willow Creek Association has provided incredible leadership in reminding the Christian community of both the benefits and necessity of small groups. Their resources are used throughout the world to help children of the King move closer to each other and to Jesus

More recently Rick Warren's *The Purpose Driven Life* has renewed this emphasis on community. Just today I read where churches across the country are committing 40 days of concentrated small group study and reflection to finding the reason God put them here.

I believe there are several reasons why small groups are becoming so popular and are so incredibly effective. First, small groups reflect the Acts 2 picture of what the Christian community should look like. Acts 2:44-47 (NLT) records:

And all the believers met together constantly and shared everything they had. They sold their possessions and shared the proceeds with those in need. They worshiped together at the Temple each day, met in homes for the Lord's Supper, and shared their meals with great joy and generosity-all the while praising God and enjoying the goodwill of all the people. And each day the Lord added to their group those who were being saved.

We should be meeting together, sharing, praising God, and enjoying the company of those whom God loves so much. The short version of the greatest two commandments, as defined by Jesus, is to love God and love each other. Small groups help us do both.

Second, small groups remind us that we are not alone. As we move closer to each other the list grows of those who love us just as we are; those we could call in the middle of the night. Life has more meaning when we are loved deeply just as we are. We are also not alone in our struggles and failures. We learn that others struggle just as we do, even those who seem to be spiritual heavyweights. Then we learn that Paul struggled, and Peter, and the list goes on and on. Interacting and building relationships with Christ followers reminds us that while we follow the perfect One we remain fallen, but loved. Loved by God, loved by each other.

Finally, small groups build a critical element into our lives that far too few of us have – accountability. In small groups we develop relationships that are so close, so pure, based on the mutual love of Jesus, that our lives become transparent. We can see right through each other. We see the pain even when it's not voiced. We hear and sense the disappointment, the elation, the anger, even the evasiveness. Small groups help us drop our masks and be who God created us to be while providing a "check and balance" when we are not living true to God.

Living the Abundant Life started as an idea, a train of thought that was the result of moving into a deeper relationship with God. Obedience to His call to write the book was the first step in the right direction. A conversation with John Perry in Jacksonville, Florida helped me realize that one of the primary goals of the book is "ink on the page" from small groups. As such, the book and Table of Contents have been structured specifically for use in small groups.

First, there are *Personal Reflections* throughout the book.

More than questions to merely consider, these are questions and issues I ask you to reflect on, write answers to, and discuss in your small group. In my experience, there is great similarity between the struggles and desires, good and bad, of people in general and Christ followers in particular. Appropriately sharing those struggles and dreams inside of trusted, Christ-centered relationships can help gain victory over the struggles and propel you in the direction of abundant living. In speaking with churches and other groups I have often felt that my only goal was to get people to work on the questions in the *Personal Reflections* section. Openness to that type of reflection, combined with the working of the Holy Spirit, is the manner in which abundant living may be found.

The *Table of Contents* also reflects the heavy emphasis on small group use and working through the *Personal Reflections*. Each of the *Personal Reflections* exercises and the corresponding page number are listed in the *Table of Contents*. The primary reason for this is so that small groups can agree on how much of the book to read, and how many of the *Personal Reflections* to work on between sections. Some groups meet weekly, some every other week, some monthly. Whatever the time period between meetings, whatever your pace in working through the material, you can discuss and agree on how much material to cover between each session. This flexibility will also permit you to get as lost in discussion as you desire without fear of falling behind – your group sets the pace and can always shift as needed. Let group dynamics and the Holy Spirit determine the pace.

Finally, I pray that you will find *Living the Abundant Life* of benefit to you and your small group. Any feedback on how you have used the book, how it has benefited you or others, your journey toward the Intersection and abundance, or recommendations for improvements or other resources is always welcome.

Please visit www.rogerweldon.com or contact me directly at roger@rogerweldon.com

Abundant blessings!

BIBLIOGRAPHICAL NOTES

Notes to Reader

1. Os Guinness, *The Call* (Word Publishing, 1998).
2. Adapted from a poem by Gerard Manley Hopkins in which he wrote: "What I do is me: for that I came."

Introduction

1. John Eldredge, *The Journey of Desire* (Thomas Nelson Publishers, 2000).

Chapter 1 – How Did this Happen?

1. John Eldredge, *The Journey of Desire* (Thomas Nelson Publishers, 2000).
2. Lin Yutang, *The Importance of Living* (John Day with Reynal & Hitchcock, 1937) after title page, statement attributed to Chang Ch'ao.
3. C.S. Lewis, *The Abolition of Man* (Harper San Francisco).
4. Charles R. Swindoll, *The Grace Awakening* (Word Publishing, 1996).
5. Bill Hybels, "The Art of Self Leadership," *Leadership Journal,* Summer 2001.
6. *The Weight of Glory*, a sermon at the church of St Mary the Virgin, Oxford, 1941. – Quoted from 'Screwtape proposes a Toast and other pieces' (Found, 1998).
7. Tommy Newberry, *Success Is Not An Accident* (Looking Glass Books, 1999).
8. John Eldredge, *The Journey of Desire* (Thomas Nelson Publishers, 2000).

Chapter 2 – What is the Alternative?

1. Barbara Sher, Barbara Smith (contributor), *I Could Do Anything If I Only Knew What It Was* (DTP, September 1995).

Chapter 3 –Passion

1. Cited from multiple sources to include "great quotations" resources
2. Henry David Thoreau, *Walden* and "Civil Disobedience" (NAL Penguin Inc., 1960)
3. John Eldredge, *The Journey of Desire* (Thomas Nelson Publishers, 2000).
4. Viktor E. Frankl, *Man's Search For Meaning* (Washington Square Press Publication of POCKET BOOKS, 1985).
5. Sermon by Dr Martin Luther King Jr., "The Drum Major Instinct," 1968

Chapter 4 –Vision

1. John Eldredge, *Wild at Heart* (Thomas Nelson, Inc, 2001).
2. Max DePree, *Leadership is an Art* (Dell Publishing, 1989).
3. Andy Stanley, *Visioneering* (Multnomah Publishers, Inc., 1999).
4. Max Lucado, *Just Like Jesus* (Word Publishing, 1998).

Chapter 5 –Gifts

1. Os Guinness, *The Call* (Word Publishing, 1998).
2. Dr Laurence J. Peter and Raymond Hull, *The Peter Principle: Why Things Always Go Wrong* (William Morrow & Company, Inc).
3. CampusCrusadeforChrist.com
4. C. Peter Wagner, *Discover Your Spiritual Gifts* (Regal Books, 2002).
5. James I Robertson, Jr., *Stonewall Jackson: The Man, The Soldier, The Legend* (Macmillan Publishing USA, 1997).
6. Billy Graham, *The Holy Spirit* (Grason, 1978).
7. Ibid.
8. "Awareness of Spiritual Gifts Is Changing," News Release from Barna Research Group, Ltd., (Ventura, CA), February 5, 2001.
9. Billy Graham, *The Holy Spirit* (Grason, 1978).
10. John Ortberg, Laurie Pederson, and Judson Poling, *Gifts: The Joy of Serving God* (Zondervan Publishing House, 2000).

Chapter 6–Intersection

1. Max DePree, *Leadership is an Art* (Dell Publishing, 1989).

2. Ronald A. Heifetz & Marty Linsky, *Leadership on the Line: Staying alive through the dangers of leading* (Harvard Business School Press, 2002).

3. Oswald Chambers, *My Utmost for His Highest* (Barbour and Company, Inc, 1963).

4. Lin Yutang, *The Importance of Living* (John Day with Reynal & Hitchcock, 1937).

ABOUT THE AUTHOR

Roger Weldon was raised in the small town of Hahira, Georgia. He joined the Navy after graduating from High School and spent six years as an enlisted cryptologic technician. He went to Jacksonville University on an NROTC scholarship, where he graduated with a degree in psychology. After college, Roger served another 4 years in the Navy aboard the guided missile destroyer USS RUSSELL (DDG-59) as a Surface Warfare Officer.

After his Navy career, Roger went to work in the banking industry. He has worked in Alabama, Florida, and Mississippi as a Branch Manager, Business Banker, and Group Sales Manager. He is currently a Senior Vice President and City President of a group of banks in Tupelo, MS.

Roger has a passion for the topic of leadership and for helping people understand the abundance that awaits them by virtue of their being a child of the King. He is an avowed "competition junkie" with a deep love of sports and a serious NASCAR fetish. Roger and his wife, Beth, have three children - Emily, Raymond, and Ethan – and routinely collect stray dogs, cats, and horses for their budding petting zoo.

Roger always welcomes feedback and dialogue on *Living the Abundant Life* and the process of claiming the life that Jesus came to provide. For more information visit www.rogerweldon.com or contact him directly at roger@rogerweldon.com

Printed in the United States
23084LVS00006B/1-51